F. SCOTT FITZGERALD

ARTHUR MIZENER

F. SCOTT
FITZGERALD

with 135 illustrations

THAMES AND HUDSON

To Bibsy & Lenny with love

Frontispiece: a hitherto unpublished
studio portrait of F. Scott Fitzgerald
when he was a Princeton undergraduate.

© *1972 Arthur Mizener*

*First published in paperback in the United
States in 1987 by Thames and Hudson Inc.,
500 Fifth Avenue,
New York, New York 10110*

*Library of Congress Catalog Card Number
86–51196*

Printed and bound in Great Britain

FRANCIS SCOTT KEY FITZGERALD was born 24 September 1896 on the edge of the best residential area of St Paul, Minnesota. His father, Edward Fitzgerald, had come to St Paul shortly after the Civil War, from Montgomery County in Maryland. On his mother's side, Edward Fitzgerald was descended from people who had lived in Montgomery County before the Revolution: Francis Scott Key was a remote cousin of his mother. He was a quiet gentlemanly man with beautiful Southern manners that perhaps left him exceptionally defenseless before the determined attack of 'Molly' McQuillan, who – according to the gossip of those days – persuaded him to propose to her by threatening to throw herself into the Mississippi.

Mary McQuillan was the eldest of the four children of Philip McQuillan, an Irish immigrant who made two fortunes in the wholesale grocery business before dying at the age of forty-four. His widow continued to occupy the imposing Victorian McQuillan mansion on St Paul's most important residential street, Summit Avenue. It represented the security and permanence of wealth to Mrs

Summit Avenue in St Paul, Minnesota, as it appeared in 1916, when Fitzgerald lived there. He later described Summit Avenue as 'a museum of American architectural failures'.

5

(*Above left*) Fitzgerald as a baby, with his mother in front of 479–480 Laurel Avenue in St Paul.

(*Above right*) as a boy.

McQuillan's small grandson, whose childhood was spent moving from place to place because of his father's inability to make a living and who could be reduced to uncontrollable terror by the news that his father had lost his job.

Nevertheless, the McQuillans did not represent breeding; they were – as Fitzgerald later put it with revealing intensity – 'straight 1850 potato-famine Irish', a fact that his mother seemed determined to advertise by her persistent eccentricity. Such money as there was, with all it suggested of security, stability, success and position, came, then, from the McQuillan side of the family. But breeding – right instincts, good manners, the need for 'honor, courtesy, courage' – a respect for which was a powerful motive throughout Fitzgerald's life, he got from his father. Nick Carroway, the narrator of *The Great Gatsby*, who represents this side of Fitzgerald's nature, has been told by his father to remember, when he is tempted to criticize others, that 'a sense of the fundamental decencies is parcelled out unequally at birth'. In *Tender Is the Night*, Dick Diver's father, a clergyman from Buffalo, New York, has taught him the need for 'good instincts' and those

Fitzgerald's mother, Mary McQuillan Fitzgerald.

Fitzgerald with his father, Edward Fitzgerald. This photograph was taken at Christmas 1899, when Fitzgerald was three.

Daniel Chester French's statue of the Christian student. He is dressed in a football uniform but has an academic robe thrown over his left shoulder and no doubt very serious books in his left hand. Until 1930, this statue stood facing the undergraduate center in Murray Dodge, with its back to the Library. It represented the official ideal of an American undergraduate in Fitzgerald's time.

(*Far left*) Sam White, captain of the Princeton football team in 1911, whose dramatic play, Fitzgerald once said, persuaded him to go to Princeton.

(*Left*) Hobey Baker, perhaps the most brilliant athlete ever to attend Princeton. He was captain of the football team in 1913, Fitzgerald's freshman year. Baker was the model for Allenby, the football captain in *This Side of Paradise.*

'eternal necessary human values' which Fitzgerald – for all that he was with some justice supposed to represent the values of the Jazz Age – believed that age fatally lacked.

When he began school, Fitzgerald quickly assimilated the conventional values of his age-group and added to the Revolutionary heroes his father had taught him to admire the American gentleman-athlete. This figure grew rapidly in his imagination with the help of the boys' books he read, from which he learned to think of this hero as a prep-school or college boy, small in size (as he was), who by some wholly unexpected display of skill and pluck won the big game for Newman or Princeton. So deeply committed did he become to this dream of glory and so determined was he to make it a reality of his life that he persisted stubbornly all through prep-school trying to become a member of the football team, despite his lack of size and talent, despite his sometimes acute physical fear. He even tried out for the freshman football team at Princeton. The ideal he had in mind is represented with almost comic perfection by the once famous statue of the Christian student by Daniel Chester French that used to stand on the Princeton campus. This ideal seemed to Fitzgerald to be realized again and again in the world around him – in Sam White who won the Princeton-Harvard football game of 1911 with a dramatic run, in the 'slim and defiant' Hobey Baker (as he was called in *This Side of Paradise*), the Princeton football captain of 1913; in 'the romantic Buzz Law whom I had last seen one cold fall twilight in

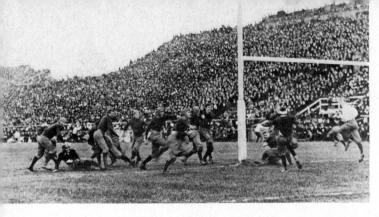

Fifteen years after the event, Fitzgerald remembered seeing 'the romantic Buzz Law . . . one cold fall twilight . . . kicking from behind his goal line with a bloody bandage round his head.' This is the Princeton-Yale game of 1913. The man blocking for the kicker is Hobey Baker.

The house at 599 Summit Avenue (*opposite*) where Fitzgerald grew up and where, in the top-story room, he wrote the final version of *This Side of Paradise*.

1915, kicking from behind his goal line with a bloody bandage round his head', the sight of whom, years later, in the Champs-Elysées, could make Fitzgerald's heart stop.

This is a characteristic example of the way Fitzgerald committed his feelings to the most brilliant of the representative people of his society and, by the sheer intensity of his feeling for them, made them into symbols – however absurdly inadequate they might seem to the eye of common sense – for the whole of experience. Fitzgerald's habit of accepting the values available in his world – largely, no doubt, because of his deep need to live out in the actual world whatever values he committed himself to – makes him, in this respect, a very conventional and representative man of his time. What is not representative is the amount of feeling he poured into whatever ideal he accepted, the sheer intensity of his commitment. By the age of twelve Fitzgerald had developed most of the conventional boyhood interests. He had fallen in love at dancing school, organized plays in a neighbor's attic, collected stamps and cigar bands, played 'guard or tackle [on neighborhood football teams] and usually scared silly', written a detective story and a history of the United States that ended with the battle of Bunker Hill, and, like the small boy in his story 'Absolution', told his first, terrifying lie at confession. He was 'by occupation actor, athlete, scholar, philatelist and collector of cigar bands'.

During the next ten years of Fitzgerald's life his family continued to move regularly, but always around the periphery of St Paul's most important residential area, that Summit Avenue Fitzgerald was later to call 'a museum of American architectural failures'. Eventually they settled in a house at 599 Summit Avenue, just about where Summit Avenue declines into a socially undistinguished street, a fact Fitzgerald felt so acutely that even with the heady self-confidence generated by the acceptance of his first novel he could report the news in a letter headed:

> (599 Summit Avenue)
> In a house below the average
> On a street above the average. . . .

Fitzgerald at the age of fifteen, when he was at Newman Academy.

Perhaps some of this feeling was justified by objective conditions. St Paul, like so many of the best cities of America in that time, certainly had a great deal of direct and unself-conscious democracy. But it also had wealth and an inherited, New England sense of social order.

At the top [Fitzgerald said later] came those whose grandparents had brought something with them from the East, a vestige of money and culture; then came the families of the big self-made merchants, the 'old settlers' of the sixties and seventies. . . . After this came certain well-to-do 'new people' – mysterious, out of a cloudy past, possibly unsound.

This was the world Fitzgerald grew up in; but he would certainly not have been so anxiously convinced that he was hovering socially on the edge of it and, as a consequence, alternated so violently between self-assertion and self-doubt had he not been so acutely aware of what he was convinced were his dubious credentials.

I am [he said long afterwards] half black Irish and half old American stock. . . . The black Irish half of the family had the money and looked down upon the

Ina Claire as she appeared in 1914 shortly after she had starred in *The Quaker Girl*, which so deeply impressed Fitzgerald when he saw it as a boarding-school student.

Maryland side of the family who . . . really had . . . 'breeding'. So . . . I spent my youth alternately crawling in front of the kitchen maids and insulting the great.

The results of this attitude showed up almost immediately when he went to St Paul Academy, where the school magazine quickly asked someone to 'poison Scotty or find some means to shut his mouth'. In his passionate effort to succeed he neglected his work so badly his family decided to send him to a boarding school in New Jersey called Newman. He looked forward to it with all the eagerness and intensity of his nature. Here was the theater he had always dreamed of, the kind of place in which the heroes of all the Ralph Henry Barbour books he had read had distinguished themselves. As a result, he made himself as unpopular at Newman as he had been at St Paul Academy. Yet almost nothing could discourage him. He worked grimly at football and on his boyish schemes for retrieving his lost popularity, suffering perhaps more than most unpopular boys because he also knew that he was 'one of the poorest boys in a rich boys' school'. His only relief was getting away to New York to see the musical comedies so popular at the time – Ina Claire in *The Quaker Girl* or Gertrude

Bryant in *Little Boy Blue*. The writing of a famous musical comedy was added to his literary ambitions, an addition that threw him with renewed fervor into the amateur theatricals of St Paul.

By his second and last year at Newman he had gradually succeeded in becoming, if not popular, at least accepted. Then during the spring of his senior year, he discovered that Princeton had an organization called the Triangle Club that produced an annual undergraduate review. 'From then on,' he once said, 'the university question was settled.' (At another time, however, he said it was the great Sam White's touchdown run against Harvard in 1911 that won him to Princeton.) In an all too characteristic and ominous way, he failed one of his entrance examinations for Princeton and was only admitted after taking the exam a second time in September. When he saw the results, he wired his mother: ADMITTED SEND FOOTBALL PADS AND SHOES IMMEDIATELY PLEASE WAIT TRUNK.

The Princeton of Fitzgerald's day was essentially an undergraduate College (though the Graduate College was dedicated the fall Fitzgerald arrived). It consisted mainly of the buildings above the transverse line set by McCosh Walk, though a few of the dormitories of the lower campus had been built. Nassau Street was unpaved and its old buildings had not yet been replaced by fake Georgian. Palmer Stadium was under construction and would first be used for the Dartmouth game of Fitzgerald's sophomore year. The student body numbered about 1500 and the library possessed a good undergraduate collection of perhaps 300,000 books. The collegiate customs of hazing

A scene from *The Coward*, produced in St Paul by the Elizabethan Dramatic Club in the summer of 1913. Fitzgerald wrote the play, appearing in a minor role, and served as stage manager.

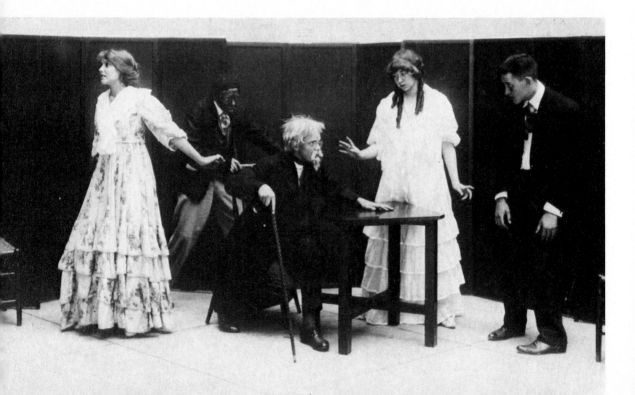

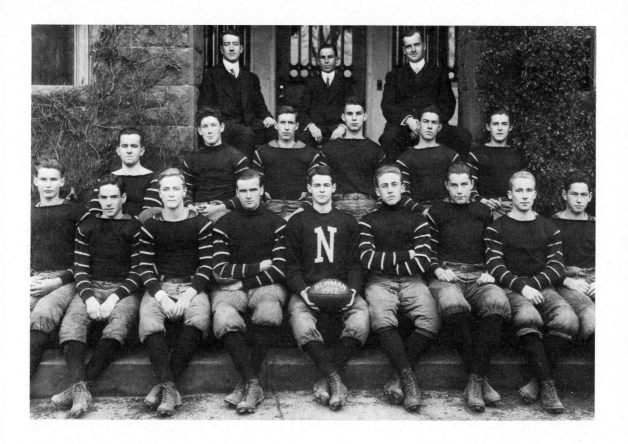

Fitzgerald (front row, third from the left) on the Newman Academy football team of 1912.

and physically violent class rivalries were rapidly fading and the fact that, in 1913, there were only six undergraduate automobiles in Princeton would soon seem astonishing. The late teens were, as Dean Gauss once said, 'the Indian Summer of the "College Customs" era in our campus life'.

It was a small world in which most of the traditions and standards of values, both social and intellectual, had come down almost unimpaired from the Nineties. '... Ernest Dowson and Oscar Wilde were the latest sensational writers who had got past the stained glass windows [of the library],' Edmund Wilson would remember later. Football was a deadly serious affair. The success or failure of a university year rested on the Yale and Harvard games, and even the sophisticated and disillusioned Fitzgerald of *This Side of Paradise* could have Amory Blaine watch a football-rally parade marching up University Avenue and observe that 'There at the head of the white platoon marched Allenby, the football captain, slim and defiant, as if aware that this year the hopes of the college rested on him, that his hundred-and-sixty pounds were expected to dodge to victory through the heavy blue and crimson lines.'

The Princeton University campus in Fitzgerald's time.

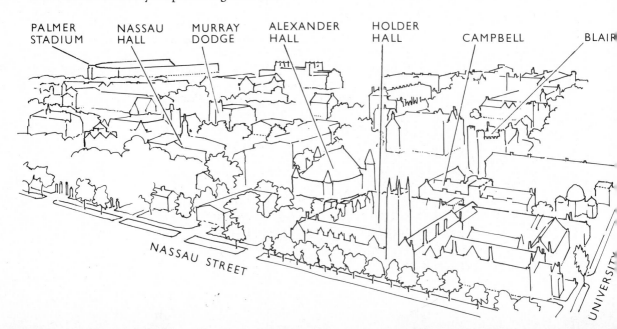

PALMER STADIUM   NASSAU HALL   MURRAY DODGE   ALEXANDER HALL   HOLDER HALL   CAMPBELL   BLAIR

NASSAU STREET

UNIVERSITY

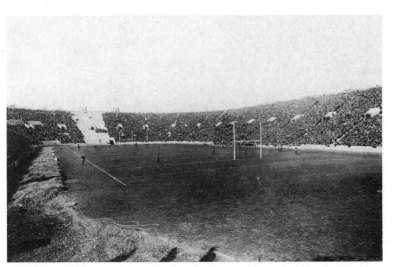

(*Above*) the arch of Blair Dormitory from the lower part of the campus.

(*Left*) Princeton *versus* Dartmouth, autumn 1914, in the game at which Palmer Stadium was dedicated. This was the autumn of Fitzgerald's sophomore year.

John Peale Bishop (*left*) and Ed‑ mund Wilson (*right*) as Princeton undergraduates. Both were good friends of Fitzgerald.

Football was obviously the best means to social distinction, as the Fitzgerald who sent his mother that telegram when he was admitted knew full well; and social distinction was the main concern of the undergraduate.

. . . nothing [as John Peale Bishop put it] matters much but that a man bear an agreeable person and maintain with slightly mature modifications the standards of prep school. Any extreme of habilement, pleasures or opinions is apt to be charac‑ terized as 'running it out', and 'to run it out' is to lose all chance of social distinction.

Besides football there were, fortunately for him, other, if less im‑ mediately profitable roads to social success, such as the Triangle Club. Energetic pursuit of these means to social distinction was duly rewarded at the club elections in the middle of the sophomore year, when everyone would be graded according to the importance of the club to which he was elected.

But if this was the dominant world of Fitzgerald's Princeton, the university was also the place where he could find himself sitting at dinner next to an aristocratic‑looking boy and be caught up in an exciting conversation with John Peale Bishop about Shaw and Meredith and *The Yellow Book*. For Princeton also had a modest intellectual world. At the end of his Princeton career, Fitzgerald would turn to this group and often in later years think of it as the only part of his life at Princeton that had had any real value.

One of the charms of Princeton was the way its two worlds managed to tolerate one another; very little of the arrogant scorn that so often divides them today seems to have existed then. One could hardly – to be sure – become a really big man without pretty well conforming to the customs of the social world and competing for the right rewards. But the *Princeton Pictorial Review*, which spoke for the conventional majority, could write radical editorials in favor of 'running it out', and Edmund Wilson, the most imposing intellectual of his Princeton generation, could write the Triangle Club's 1915–16 show, called *The Evil Eye*, what Dean Gauss called with obvious amusement 'the most serious of all his literary *péchés de jeunesse*'. Fitzgerald wrote the lyrics for *The Evil Eye*.

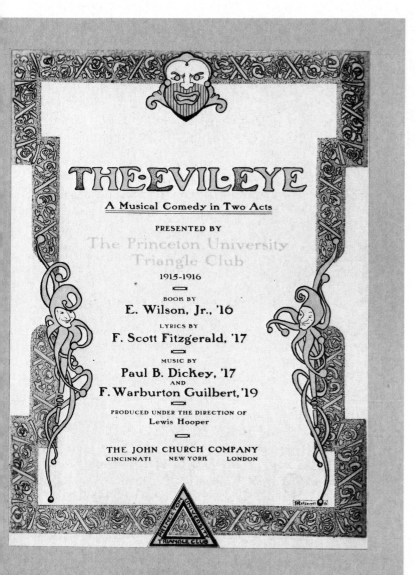

Cover of the musical score for *The Evil Eye*, the Princeton Triangle Club show for 1915–16, written by Edmund Wilson with lyrics by Fitzgerald.

The Court of Holder, where
Edmund Wilson lived as an
undergraduate.

It is typical of the kind of tolerance the social world had for the
intellectual that Fitzgerald, very much a member of the social world,
should have thought of Edmund Wilson as 'the shy little scholar of
Holder Court'. It is equally typical of the intellectual world's view of
the social that Wilson should have remembered his first meeting with
Fitzgerald as he did.

note the haughty expression

Fitzgerald and Jimmy Dunn, an undergraduate friend. The inscription is in Fitzgerald's hand.

I climbed, a quarter-century and more
Played out, the college steps, unlatched my door,
And, creature strange to college, found you there,
The pale skin, hard green eyes, and yellow hair –
Intently pinching out before a glass
Some pimples left by parties at the Nass. . . .

For Fitzgerald had begun his career at Princeton by plunging into the competition for social success, 'where,' as he would later say, with all the ambivalence of his divided feelings about life, 'all the petty snobbishness within the prep-school, all the caste system of Minneapolis, all were . . . magnified, glorified and transformed into a

Fitzgerald as a Princeton under-graduate in 1915.

glittering classification.' Princeton, he thought, was the university where the gentlemen of American society congregated – as distinguished from Yale, where the ambitious went, and Harvard, the home of the professional intellectuals. As with Dexter Green of 'Winter Dreams', to whom he would ascribe so many of his own feelings, '[His winter dreams] persuaded [him] . . . to pass up a business course at the State university . . . for the precarious advantages of attending an older more famous university in the East, where he was bothered by his scanty funds. . . . He wanted not association with glittering things and glittering people – he wanted the glittering things themselves. Often he reached out for the best without knowing why he wanted it.'

The seventeen-year-old Fitzgerald who arrived at Princeton in 1913 was a small boy, five-seven and one hundred and thirty-eight pounds, slight and slope-shouldered. With his yellow hair and green eyes he was almost girlishly handsome. He concentrated that almost terrifying imaginative energy of his on the Princeton style, transforming it, at least for himself, into an image of the good life; it made him stick out among conventional Princeton gentlemen, an odd and unusual person. Moreover, he could not conceal the motive for all this conformity, as he was supposed to. 'I want to pull strings . . . or be Princetonian chairman or Triangle President. I want to be admired,' says Amory Blaine in *This Side of Paradise*. So did Fitzgerald.

In October he went out for the Triangle Club and worked hard at small tasks for that year's show; by February he was at work on a libretto for the next year's show. By then he was also in serious academic difficulties; when the midyear grades were reported he had failed three subjects, barely passed three others, and achieved mediocre respectability in one – English. The experience must have frightened him, or perhaps he had more time free from more pressing engagements during the spring; in any event, he flunked only one more course in the spring term and, by tutoring that summer, was able to return for his sophomore year in precarious 'good standing'.

During that spring, too, Father Fay, a Catholic convert who had taken Fitzgerald up when he was a student at Newman, had invited him out to dinner and had him down for a socially dazzling week-end on the Jersey shore. Father Fay came of a wealthy family and was a man of taste and some cultivation, an aesthete and dandy who loved perfume and epigrams. He gave Fitzgerald a glimpse of a world that was at once luxurious and civilized and that was also Catholic without being dreary and puritanical as the Catholicism of his youth in St Paul had been. Until Father Fay died in the influenza epidemic of 1919, his influence on Fitzgerald was considerable; how much Fitzgerald admired him is evident from the portrait of him as Father Darcy in *This Side of Paradise* and from the fact that Fitzgerald dedicated the book to him – even though he did misspell Father Fay's first name, '. . . the jovial, impressive prelate who could dazzle an embassy ball, and the green-eyed, intent youth . . . accepted in their own minds a relation of father and son within a half-hour's conversation,' Fitzgerald wrote in *This Side of Paradise*; and if Fay's letters, with their 'Dear Old Boy's' and their second-rate Nineties epigrams hardly support this view of him, Fitzgerald's description nonetheless shows the ideal Fitzgerald wanted him to fulfill. Father Fay was the first influence to bring out in Fitzgerald – in however crude a form – those aristocratic and intellectual ideals that perhaps had always lain concealed in his Southern inheritance and would be his strongest support in the dark days of his life.

That summer of 1914, between bouts of tutoring for make-up

(*Above*) the second act scene of *Fie!
Fie! Fi-Fi!*, the Triangle Club's
production for 1914–15. (*Right*) the
cover of the musical score. Fitzgerald
wrote the book as well as the lyrics
for this production.

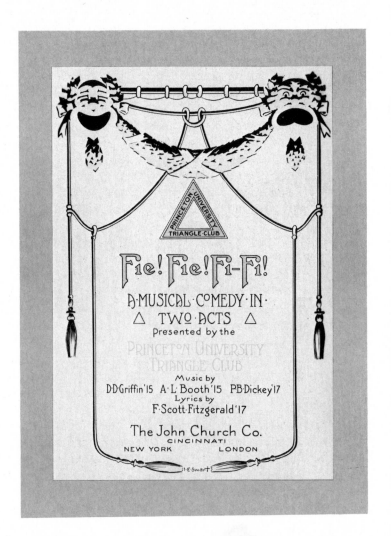

Publicity photograph of Fitzgerald as a chorus girl for *The Evil Eye*. This photograph was widely reproduced but Fitzgerald never appeared in *The Evil Eye* because he got into academic difficulties. This cut appeared in the rotogravure section of *The New York Times*.

examinations in the courses he had failed that year, he found time to write and produce another play for St Paul's Elizabethan Dramatic Club. But this production brought his dramatic career to an abrupt and dismaying halt, for back at Princeton he discovered that, despite his 'Good Standing', the Faculty Committee on Non-Athletic Organizations felt him academically too insecure to be eligible to participate in that year's Triangle show, even though he was to be cast as one of the leading 'Show Girls' and figured prominently in the Triangle's early publicity photographs. His ineligibility was all the more severe a blow because the Triangle Club that September

The Nassau Literary Magazine

VOLUME LXXII   FEBRUARY   No. 7

THE SPIRE AND THE GARGOYLE

I

The night mist fell. From beyond the moon it rolled, clustered about the spires and towers, and then settled below them so that the dreaming peaks seemed still in lofty aspiration toward the stars. Figures that dotted the daytime like ants now brushed along as ghosts in and out of the night. Even the buildings seemed infinitely more mysterious as they loomed suddenly out of the darkness, outlined each by a hundred faint squares of yellow light. Indefinitely from somewhere a bell boomed the quarter hour and one of the squares of light in an east campus recitation hall was blotted out for an instant as a figure emerged. It paused and resolved itself into a boy who stretched his arms wearily, and advancing threw himself down full length on the damp grass by the sun-dial. The cool bathed his eyes and helped to force away the tiresome picture of what he had just left, a picture that, in the two strenuous weeks

(*Above*) opening page of Fitzgerald's story for *The Nassau Literary Magazine* for February 1917. The story is about the stupidity of an institution that would deprive a student of extra-curricular honors because of academic failure.

accepted the libretto he had been working on (though Walker Ellis, the President of the club, put his own name to it, leaving Fitzgerald credit only for the lyrics).

In a way that would be comic if it had not been so serious a matter to Fitzgerald, he was almost more puzzled than angry that anything so obviously important to his social career at Princeton as his success with the Triangle Club could be interfered with by the academic authorities. Almost at once he wrote a story about this experience called 'The Spire and the Gargoyle'. The spire represents the imitation Gothic architecture of Princeton that stands for the romance of social success there; the gargoyle is the instructor on whom passing his make-up examination depended. The point of the story is the absurd irony of a superior person like Fitzgerald finding himself at the mercy of this academic worm. In spite of his bitter disappointment at being prevented from playing a part in the show, Fitzgerald characteristically threw himself into the work of producing it. Then he went sadly home for Christmas instead of on the tour that carried the Triangle Club across America in a haze of alcohol and debutantes.

But back in St Paul he found that 'Midge' Hersey had brought home

with her for the vacation her roommate at Westover School, a celebrated beauty from Chicago named Ginevra King, and everyone –
including the principals – supposed the man likely to interest her was
Fitzgerald, whose prestige had risen greatly with his success at Princeton
and who was known to be a man who 'drank'. A mutual attraction
was almost inevitable under these circumstances. For Ginevra,
Fitzgerald was at best the first among equals, of whom there were a
great many. But for Fitzgerald, Ginevra was a revelation. She moved
through the world with the ease and assurance of a lifetime of wealth,
of social position taken for granted, of parties and proms she had
always dominated as if by divine prerogative. Fitzgerald later put
much of what he felt her to be into Judy Jones, the heroine of 'Winter
Dreams'. She seemed to him – as Daisy Fay did to Jay Gatsby –
'extraordinary, but he didn't realize [until he knew her well] just how
extraordinary a "nice" girl could be.'

What struck him most was her effortless ease; to Fitzgerald, with
his genteel poverty, his social uncertainty, his puritanical Irish
capacity for anticipating disaster, there was something of a miracle
about this. Here was a girl who conquered everyone as a matter

(*Left*) the St Paul Town and
Country Club in 1915, the year
when Fitzgerald met Ginevra King
there.

(*Right*) Ginevra King as she
appeared when Fitzgerald met her.
This photograph belonged to
Fitzgerald.

Ginevra King when
Fitzgerald knew her, about
1915.

of course, and who yet remained essentially untouched, free. The
serious moralist in him, the good side of his puritanical nature, could
sense the danger for someone who was so sure she could enjoy all the
pleasures and sexual victories open to a beautiful girl and then, in due
course, settle into some permanent though no less romantic future.
'The future vista of her life', he wrote of her in *This Side of Paradise*,
'seemed an unending succession of scenes like this: under moonlight
and pale starlight, and in the backs of warm limousines and in low,
cosy roadsters stopped under sheltering trees – only the boy might
change. . . .'

Here, for the first time in an actual girl, Fitzgerald found the ideal
girl whose image had been developing in his imagination and whom
he would, without any conscious intention of starting a social revolution, later make the ideal girl of his generation. Ginevra gave sub-
stance to an ideal Fitzgerald would cling to for a lifetime; to the end
of his days, the thought of her could bring tears to his eyes. In a way

The Pyne estate, where Fitzgerald and John Peale Bishop used to take long walks to discuss poetry.

that was very characteristic of him and, at least on the face of it, in-consistent with the hedonism of the Twenties, he remained devoted to Ginevra as long as she would allow him to, writing her daily the incoherent, expressive letters all young lovers write: '. . . Oh, it's hard to write you what I really *feel* when I think of you so much; you've gotten to mean to me a *dream* that I can't put on paper any more. . . .'

When he took the examinations at midyear he managed to pass all but one subject and thus make himself eligible for club elections that spring, and in March he chose, from the four clubs that sent him bids, Cottage Club, the 'Big Four' club that was most committed to the ideal of the fashionable gentleman. At the club party to celebrate the

The back porch of Fitzgerald's Princeton club, Cottage, as it appeared in his time. Here Fitzgerald and Edmund Wilson used to sit through long spring evenings talking about literature.

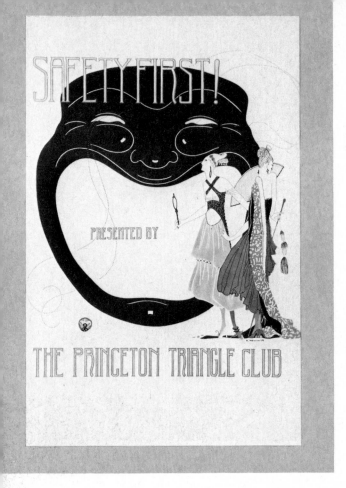

The third of the Triangle Club productions for which Fitzgerald wrote the lyrics, *Safety First*, 1916–17. The book for the show was written by John Biggs, Fitzgerald's roommate and later a distinguished judge.

election of new members he passed out cold for the first time in his life. That spring he was also elected secretary of the Triangle Club and put on the editorial board of the campus humor magazine, *The Tiger*. He felt confident – with some reason – that in due course he would become president of the Triangle Club and a member of the Senior Council.

In the ebullience created by these successes, he again forgot about the gargoyle, and that spring he failed three more subjects; when he returned in the fall, he failed two of the three make-up examinations. His situation was now serious. He simply could not afford to be ineligible this term, when the elections for the offices he had set his heart on and had all but won would be held. But he was. With his characteristic determination in the face of adversity, he hung on for a month or so, hoping for a miracle. Then in November he caught malaria, which was more or less endemic in Princeton with its swamps and mosquitoes. This illness gave him an excuse for leaving college before the midyear examinations, when he was almost certain to flunk out. '. . . it took them', he said with unabated bitterness twenty-five years later, 'four months to take it all away from me – stripped of every office and on probation – the phrase was "ineligible for extra-curricular activities", . . . There were to be no badges of pride, no medals after all. It seemed . . . that I had lost every single thing I wanted.'

Though from any objective point of view these were trivial disappointments, they were one of the great blows of Fitzgerald's life, something he never forgot. He had committed his feelings to the life of Princeton, and the value of success in that life depended for him on those feelings, not on its objective value. He brought to Princeton for redemption all the uncertainties and defeats of his early life. To have succeeded at Princeton would have wiped them all out. He had succeeded there; but just as he was about to be admitted to the life of success, to know what it was to feel wholly at ease in a world that – at least before he had entered it – he thought would satisfy all his sense of splendor, the door was shut in his face.

He spent eight unhappy months before returning to Princeton the next fall writing yet another libretto for the Triangle Club (it was rejected) and making an unhappy trip to Lake Forest to see Ginevra. 'Poor boys', he was told, 'shouldn't think of marrying rich girls'; in

Lake Forest, a fashionable summer resort for Chicago people, as it appeared in 1916. Here Fitzgerald spent a last unhappy time with Ginevra King that summer.

(*Left*) Henry Strater as a Princeton undergraduate.

(*Above*) David Bruce, later a distinguished diplomat, when he was an undergraduate at Princeton.

any event Ginevra was tiring of Fitzgerald's importunities, and when he returned to Princeton, they separated for good. Back at Princeton his interests – perhaps perforce – began to shift. He was still ineligible, and though he wrote songs for that year's Triangle show, his heart was really not in it. He began to see a great deal of John Peale Bishop and John Biggs, who, in March, succeeded Bishop as editor of the *Nassau Lit*. He made friends with David Bruce and Richard Cleveland – Grover Cleveland's son – and Henry Strater, who read Tolstoy and Edward Carpenter and Walt Whitman. Strater was a revelation to him, a man wholly unaffected by the requirements of social prestige, who went about simply doing what he thought right. Here was a new conception of superiority, based on moral and intellectual integrity. Fitzgerald could never commit himself to it entirely, because he could not sacrifice the actual realization, in the world, of the life he dreamed of. But for the first time he felt the force and dignity in a rejection of the world of power.

If this shift of interest was influenced by the company he was keeping, by his delight in the life he found the freshly graduated Edmund Wilson living in Greenwich Village – so like, he felt, the life in Compton Mackenzie's enchanting *Sinister Street* – and the novel ideas of people like Strater, it was also the result of a habit that would endure all Fitzgerald's life. It was almost a necessity for him to try to come imaginatively to terms with any major experience. Instinctively, after his first academic crisis, he had attempted, in 'The Spire and the Gargoyle', to explain to himself what had happened. Now, after this final defeat by the gargoyle and his loss of Ginevra, he did the same thing. The stories he wrote for the *Nassau Lit* during this time are attempts to deal with himself and Ginevra – naive in attitude, second-hand in situation, and intensely alive with the remembered feelings of his actual experience.

This was to be the characteristic pattern of his relation to experience for the rest of his life. Within him there was a romantic, enthusiastic young man eager to plunge into life and to spend himself without counting the cost. Within him, too, was what he would call, in his notes for *Tender Is the Night*, a 'spoiled priest' who was distressed by the romantic young man's extravagant waste of his resources, both monetary and emotional, and found this extravagance tasteless. It was the spoiled priest who had seriously considered calling his novel *Trimalchio in West Egg* instead of *The Great Gatsby*. It is the tension between these two selves that gives Fitzgerald's work its distinction. If that work owes its moral force to the spoiled priest, it owes the felt experience, without which that moral force would be objectless, to the romantic young man's personal experience: the spoiled priest's 'divine' was, as T. E. Hulme once put it, 'life at its intensest'. 'Taking things hard – from Ginevra to Joe Mank –' Fitzgerald said in his notebooks: 'That's the stamp that goes into my books so that people can read it blind like brail.' (Joseph Mankiewicz was the Hollywood producer who had, Fitzgerald thought, ruined the best script he had ever written.)

This first burst of creative activity was, characteristically, followed by a reawakening of the man of action in Fitzgerald. All during that spring of 1917 Princeton had been growing more and more preoccupied with the war. In June, Fay had him down for another week-end to propose he go along on a highly secret and altogether implausible expedition to Russia. In July, he also took the examination for an army commission, and when Fay's scheme finally collapsed, he returned to Princeton to begin a restless senior year. When his commission finally came through, he was glad to leave Princeton for Fort Leavenworth. Partly because of the influence of his intellectual friends, many of whom were pacifists, and because, as he said, 'I'm too Irish for that,' Fitzgerald scorned the conventionally patriotic attitude; at the same time, his romantic nature responded enthusiastically to the idea of the heroic

Christian Gauss, a Professor of Romance Literature at Princeton and later Dean of the College. He was deeply admired by intellectual under-graduates like Fitzgerald and Edmund Wilson.

individual gallantly confronting danger. He never ceased to regret the bad luck that prevented his getting overseas during the war; it was an important experience missed.

He felt his departure from Princeton was the end of youth. 'God!' he said, 'how I miss my youth.' This was not so absurd an attitude at twenty-one as it sounds. What he was worrying about – as he continued to for the rest of his life – was his feeling that, with only a limited supply of emotional capital, he was being forced, with the end of youth, to invest it heavily; he dreaded the necessity, fearing the bad investments he knew he was bound to make.

This fresh commitment to the life of action did not mean an end to his writing career. Before he left Princeton, he showed Dean Gauss the complete manuscript of a novel that attempted to deal with the whole of his experience at Princeton. Dean Gauss persuaded him not to try to publish it. This was a blow, and as he always did when he was hit

A typical recruiting poster of the First World War.

Fitzgerald clowning with May Steiner, a Montgomery, Alabama, girl of whom he saw a good deal when he was first stationed at Camp Sheridan, before he met Zelda Sayre in September 1918.

New York's 69th Infantry entraining
for the coast and departure for
Europe, 1917.

hard, Fitzgerald came up fighting. All through his training he worked
on this book. He finished it again in the spring of 1918, but in the fall
Scribner's turned it down, and Fitzgerald returned to his career as
what a contemporary once called 'the world's worst second lieutenant'.
In June 1919, this career took him to Camp Sheridan, near Montgomery, Alabama. There, at a country club dance in September, he
met and fell in love with Zelda Sayre, the eighteen-year-old daughter

of an Alabama Supreme Court judge. She was a fascinating girl with marvelous red-gold hair and a personality of great distinction. The security of her home, which depended a good deal on the Judge's firm character and the security of the small-town society of Montgomery, both challenged her natural rebelliousness and gave her the confidence to respond to it. It was not until she had lost that security that she recognized how necessary it was to her; '... she hadn't', says the auto-biographical heroine of her novel *Save Me the Waltz*, 'been absolutely sure of how to go about anything since her marriage had precluded the Judge's resented direction.'

Wartime Montgomery, with the sudden influx of officers from all over the country that made it an almost perfect model of the social changes the war was causing everywhere, became the ideal theater for the Zelda Sayre who wanted to be a law unto herself and had the confidence to do anything she felt like doing.

The Flapper [as she put it later] . . . bobbed her hair, put on her choicest pair of earrings and a great deal of audacity and rouge and went into battle. She flirted because it was fun to flirt and wore a one-piece bathing suit because she had a good figure, she covered her face with paint and powder because she didn't need it. . . . She was conscious that the things she did were the things she had always wanted to do.

She and Fitzgerald fell deeply in love; it was a large investment of emotional capital for Fitzgerald and when, one night, as Gatsby did Daisy, he took her, 'He felt married to her, that was all'; he would never cease to feel so.

> Still does your hair's gold light the ground
>   And dazzle the blind till their old ghosts rise? . . .
> Part of a song, a remembered glory,
>   Kisses, a lazy street — and night.

Camp Sheridan, Alabama, during the First World War when Fitzgerald was stationed there as an aide-de-camp to General A. J. Ryan.

37

Zelda Sayre as she looked at the time she and Fitzgerald met in 1918 when she was eighteen.

(*Opposite*) Fitzgerald as aide-de-camp to General A. J. Ryan in 1918. The inscription, for a cousin, is in Fitzgerald's hand.

Nevertheless it was not, from the start, an easy relation. They both believed in their sovereign rights as individuals and, despite the depths of their feelings, were reluctant to commit themselves. '... except for sexual recklessness,' Fitzgerald wrote later, still shocked by Zelda's yielding to him, 'Zelda was cagey about throwing in her lot with me before I was a money-maker.' She wanted a largeness of life that neither of them had yet known and Fitzgerald respected her determination to get it; it was what he wanted too.

38

Sally Pope Taylor
from
Scott F Fitzgerald

(*Left*) Zelda, age fifteen, in ballet costume.

(*Above*) a specially posed photograph of Zelda entitled 'Folly', 1919.

(*Below*) Montgomery, Alabama, about 1919.

In October 1919 it looked for a moment as if he were 'going to get over'. Early in November his unit were sent to Camp Mills on Long Island. But there there were the usual delays. Out of boredom he got into a lot of trouble. When he was caught in a room at the Astor Hotel with a completely naked girl, and escaped from the house detective by a trick, he was saved from the police only by his commanding officer's putting him in arrest at Camp Mills. He escaped from that confinement too and when, at the armistice, his unit started back to Montgomery, he reappeared at Washington with a girl on each arm and a bottle in his hand. Back in Montgomery he renewed his courtship of Zelda, who alternately included him in the family's Christmas dinner and deserted him to go to proms at Auburn and Georgia Tech. When this happened Fitzgerald would fly into a jealous rage, get drunk, and pick a quarrel, during which Zelda usually suggested she doubted he would ever make enough money to marry her.

Wall Street on Armistice Day, 11 November 1918.

(*Above*) Fitzgerald and Zelda Sayre outside the Sayres' house in Montgomery, 1919.

(*Right*) table of contents for *The Smart Set* of November 1919, showing Fitzgerald's 'The Débutante', which he later used as a chapter in *This Side of Paradise*. It is one of his many descriptions of Zelda.

THE SMART SET
A MAGAZINE OF CLEVERNESS

The entire contents of this magazine are protected by copyright in all countries and must not be reprinted.

Editor—J. W. MILNE

NOVEMBER, 1919

Annual Subscription, 15/- post free.   Foreign Subscription, 16/- post free.

Published by THE ROLLS HOUSE PUBLISHING CO., LTD., Breams Buildings, E.C., for the Proprietor, J. W. Da Costa.

"The Smart Set" Magazine, Dane's Inn House, 265 Strand, W.C. 2 to which all editorial and advertising matter should be addressed.

Zelda Sayre in February 1920, shortly before she and Fitzgerald were married.

The minute his discharge came through, in February, he hastened to New York, where his first act was to send Zelda an encouraging telegram: ... WHILE I FEEL SURE OF YOU[R] LOVE EVERY-THING IS POSSIBLE I AM IN THE LAND OF AMBITION AND SUCCESS. In that fabled land he then tramped the streets without success in search of a job, eventually taking an ill-paid and boring one writing advertising slogans. He thought of this as only temporary, struggling doggedly nights to write short stories that would bring him fame and fortune. 'No one bought them, no one sent personal letters. I had one hundred and twenty-two rejection slips pinned in a frieze about my room.' Meanwhile Zelda was growing more and more 'nervous' wondering if she was not losing her last chance to marry some financially better-equipped admirer. In June things reached a

Childe Hassam's painting of Fifth Avenue dressed in flags for Allies Day, May 1917. 'There had been a great war fought and won and the great city of the conquering people was crossed with triumphal arches and vivid with thrown flowers of white, red, and rose,' Fitzgerald wrote a little later in 'May Day'.

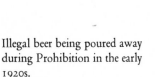

Illegal beer being poured away during Prohibition in the early 1920s.

Charles Scribner's Sons' offices at 597 Fifth Avenue as they appeared in the 1920s when Scribner's was publishing Fitzgerald, Hemingway, and Thomas Wolfe.

crisis and though Fitzgerald made a desperate trip to Montgomery to try to make her change her mind, she refused to go on with the engagement. It was not until they were re-engaged a year later that Fitzgerald was able to face up to this catastrophe squarely and make out of the experience of these months the greatest of his early stories, 'May Day'.

Now he came back to New York and went on a tremendous drunk that was brought to an end only by the advent of Prohibition. Then he took stock, and, with his characteristic impulse to come off the floor fighting and gamble on his ability to deliver a finishing punch, he quit his job, returned to St Paul, and rewrote the novel Scribner's had turned down two years before. He worked hard that summer in his hot third-floor room at 599 Summit Avenue and was able to send Scribner's the manuscript at the beginning of September. With what must surely be record alacrity for a publisher, they accepted the book two weeks later. Fitzgerald's confidence revived. He assured Scribner's that he would be content with the sale of a mere 20,000 copies of the book, shot off letters announcing his success in every direction, and promptly started another novel – 'A very ambitious novel . . . which will probably take a year', apparently his idea of almost unbelievably slow work. He also produced – between September and December – nine stories, which he found he could now sell, thanks to the acceptance of his novel. Their sale made him a man of means and in November he felt ready to return to Montgomery. Everything was the same – except that for Fitzgerald, with his melodramatic sense of time and change, nothing ever could be the same.

There was nothing changed [as he put it in one of the stories he later wrote about this part of his life] – only everything was changed. . . . He saw [the Sayres' sitting room] was only a room, and not the enchanted chamber where he had passed those poignant hours . . . that boy of fifteen months before had had something, a trust, a warmth that was gone forever.

'. . . don't', said Zelda, who understood all this, 'mourn for a poor little forlorn memory. . . . I know it's depriving you of an idea that horrifies and fascinates – you're so morbidly exaggerative. . . .'
    'I'm almost sure I'll get married as soon as my book is out', he told Maxwell Perkins, his editor at Scribner's, with his unintentionally ironic precision. This much assured, he then went to New York to arrange for an agent for his short stories. By a miracle of good luck this turned out to be a young man named Harold Ober who then worked at Paul Reynolds. He was the only agent Fitzgerald ever had, as Maxwell Perkins was the only editor he ever had. In almost no time, Ober had sold three stories – two of them revisions of previously rejected ones – for $1400. The celebrations called for by these successes and the Christmas parties in St Paul left Fitzgerald in such a nervously depressed state that – with a hypochondriacal anxiety that was to become characteristic of him – he decided he had tuberculosis and went to New Orleans for a rest. He disliked New Orleans and got nowhere with his new novel, but he kept on turning out short stories and reporting to Zelda exactly how much each had earned. He was drunk with the excitement of money and at the same time outraged by his recognition of its terrible, irrational power.

. . . the man with the jingle of money in his pocket who married the girl a year later [he always remembered] would always cherish an abiding distrust, an animosity, toward the leisure class – not the conviction of a revolutionist but the smouldering hatred of a peasant. In the years since I have never been able . . . to stop thinking that at one time a sort of *droit de seigneur* might have been exercised to give one of them my girl.

On 26 March 1920, *This Side of Paradise* was published. It hit like a bombshell. 'My, how that boy Fitzgerald can write!' said Harry

46

Max Perkins, the great editor, who got Fitzgerald's first novel, *This Side of Paradise*, published by Scribner's by making sure Mr Scribner did not read it until it was in print; he then remained Fitzgerald's editor for the rest of his career.

Hansen, more or less speaking for everybody. *This Side of Paradise* is not a great book or even, by ordinary critical standards, a very good one. Fitzgerald's old friend Edmund Wilson said of it quite truly that it was 'very immaturely imagined . . . always just verging on the ludi‑crous. . . . And . . . one of the most illiterate books of any merit ever published.' Its real strength was its naive genuineness. Fitzgerald responded with enthusiasm to the effort of his generation to live more fully and happily than their parents had and to their belief that they were being more honest and less hypocritical in doing so. These were his views too, and with that honesty of his, which, however naive it might be, had the reality of a great gift behind it, he could make the youthful world he described – no matter how unable he was to judge it maturely – hauntingly and embarrassingly real, could make a kind of American folk ballad out of it, as he once literally did.

VANITY FAIR

There'd be an orchestra
 Bingo! Bango!
Playing for us
  To dance the tango,
And people would clap
  When we arose,
At her sweet face
  And my new clothes.

(*Above left*) cover for *Vanity Fair*, December 1927. *Vanity Fair* probably came as close to representing the ethos of its time as any magazine ever has.

(*Above right*) the Fitzgeralds in February 1921, during the first year of their marriage.

Behind all the illiteracies, the errors of narrative relevance, the clumsiness of structure in *This Side of Paradise*, there remains this kind of genuineness. 'A lot of people thought it was a fake,' Fitzgerald said long after, 'and perhaps it was, and a lot of others thought it was a lie, which it was not.'

Fitzgerald and Zelda were to be married in New York. Zelda – though she would not admit it – was frightened of the great world of New York and kept putting off coming, but by wiring that he would BE AWFULLY NERVOUS UNTIL IT IS OVER and that the FIRST EDITION OF THE BOOK IS SOLD OUT . . . LOVE Fitzgerald

48

persuaded her to arrive in time to be married on 3 April. Their honeymoon consisted of a round of theaters and parties in New York and Princeton. At the theater they laughed loudly and deliberately at the wrong place to make the actors cross; at the Princeton house-parties Fitzgerald solemnly introduced Zelda to everyone as his mistress: their condition was such that not everyone was sure it wasn't true, especially after she had danced spectacularly on the dinner table. When they moved from their honeymoon cottage at the Biltmore to the Commodore, they celebrated the occasion by whirling about in the revolving door for half an hour. This was the beginning of the Jazz Age.

The Cascades, the dining room of the Biltmore Hotel, as it appeared in the early 1920s.

49

(*Above*) Clara Bow, the 'It Girl' as Elinor Glyn called her, Hollywood's image of the age's flaming youth, as she appeared in the early 1920s.

(*Right*) J. L. Holton's cover for *Life*, 2 June 1927. The man's clothes are caricatured but the girl's are fairly accurate.

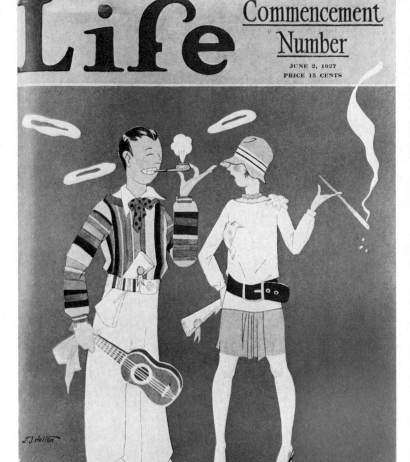

Life

Commencement Number

JUNE 2, 1927
PRICE 15 CENTS

"Now what shall we commence?"

(*Above*) a publicity photograph for a Charleston competition in New York in 1926.

(*Left*) a John Held, Jr. drawing of young people sitting on the stairs at a fraternity dance. It was drawn in 1925 and called, ironically, 'The Dance-Mad Younger Set'.

The Plaza Hotel as it appeared from Central Park in the 1920s. The Plaza was the favorite hotel of the period. It was inevitable that Gatsby, Nick Carroway, and the Buchanans should go there on the fatal Sunday when Gatsby's dream of a life with Daisy was shattered.

It was a time, as Fitzgerald pointed out in 'Early Success', when few doubted that 'America was going on the greatest, gaudiest spree in history. . . . The whole golden boom was in the air.' It was not that these young people were without social generosity or political idealism, but as Fitzgerald said after it was all over, '. . . in spite of the fact that now we are all rummaging around in our trunks wondering where the hell we left the liberty cap – "I know I *had* it" – and the moujik blouse . . . it was characteristic of the Jazz Age that it had no interest in politics at all.' Amory Blaine was, for what it was worth, a socialist. So were they all; they were sickened by the solemn hypocrisies of politicians and professional moralists. But public affairs seemed remote, and so hope-lessly absurd as to leave any sane man helpless. H. L. Mencken com-pared the superior intellectual in America to a man in a zoo. The only thing for a reasonable man to do in these circumstances, it seemed to

The telephone became a routine part of life in the Twenties, as the passage quoted in the text from Zelda's *Save Me the Waltz* shows.

them, was to concentrate on doing what was fun, 'interesting'. Practically this meant parties, and for a few years, until people began to say, like Dick Diver, 'So much fun – so long ago', life became for people like the Fitzgeralds an almost continuous party.

'We're having some people,' everybody said to everybody else 'and we want you to join us,' and they said, 'We'll telephone.'
All over New York people telephoned. They telephoned from one hotel to another to people on other parties that they couldn't get there – that they were engaged. It was always tea-time or late at night.

So Zelda remembered it when she wrote her novel ten years later.
For the young people who found *This Side of Paradise* an expression of all they felt, Fitzgerald was, in Glenway Wescott's phrase, 'a kind of king of our American youth'. On the surface anyhow, he looked the part. He was handsome and casually graceful; he loved to be

BERENICE'S MOTHER BOBS HER HAIR
Oh see the nice old la-dy and her daugh-ter. Is the nice old la-dy wild? Yes, the nice old la-dy is wild. She has been read-ing "This Side of Par-a-dise". What a pi-ty! What is het daugh-ter say-ing? She is saying "All right, Mo-ther, go on and bob your hair. Look like Min-nie the Train-ed Seal if you want to"

This cartoon appeared in *Vanity Fair* in July 1921. It parodies both Fitzgerald's short story, 'Berenice Bobs Her Hair', which appeared in *The Saturday Evening Post* on 1 May 1920, and the *Post*'s illustrations for the story. It was no doubt the success of *This Side of Paradise* that led *Vanity Fair* to print this parody.

popular and blossomed with success; he had a highly developed sense of social responsibility and always worked hard to make any occasion happy. He seemed, in his own person, a triumphant justification of the life style his book recommended. So too did Zelda, who seemed, as one of their friends put it, 'a barbarian princess from the South'.

None had such promise then, and none
Your scapegrace wit or your disarming grace;
For you were bold as was Danaë's son,
Conceived like Perseus in a dream of gold,

(*Left*) the Pulitzer Fountain in front of the Plaza Hotel at Fifth Avenue and 58th Street as it appeared in 1916. (*Above*) the same scene in a drawing by Hugh Ferriss for *Vanity Fair*, February 1922. Out of sheer ebullience Fitzgerald one day jumped, dead sober, into the Pulitzer Fountain.

John Peale Bishop said of Fitzgerald. For quite a while they managed, like young and unhaunted Divers, to play these roles with success and happiness, with what one of their friends called 'an almost theatrical innocence'.

But their life was expensive. 'It costs more', Zelda said, 'to ride on the tops of taxis . . . [and] Joseph Urban skies are expensive when they're real.' In spite of the fact that Fitzgerald had made better than $18,000 in 1920, he had already begun his lifelong practice of borrowing from both Harold Ober and Scribner's. He couldn't stop either

himself or Zelda from spending money with foolish extravagance,
but he fully understood the cost of doing so, the extent to which, all
his life, he was 'crippled . . . by my inability to handle money'.
Fitzgerald did not really care enough about money to handle it well.
What he did care about was the mobility and grace, available only to
the rich, that seemed to him necessary to the achievement of the good
life he could so vividly imagine. Not only could he find nothing to
interest him in the making of money; he seriously distrusted the process,
as he shows by sympathizing with Gatsby, who was an immensely

Studio portrait of Zelda in 1921. She used to call this her
'Elizabeth Arden face'.

successful but illegal entrepreneur, against Tom Buchanan, whose
money was perfectly legal and perfectly unearned. But if Fitzgerald
deeply admired the rich who took advantage of their wealth to live the
fully imagined life – as a few of his heroes like Gerald Murphy and
Tommy Hitchcock seemed to him to do – he scorned the merely rich.
'The idea of the grand dame slightly tight', he said, '. . . is one of the
least impressive in the world. You know: "The Foreign Office will
hear about this, hic!"' What Fitzgerald cherished was Jay Gatsby's
'heightened sensitivity to the promises of life', Dick Diver's 'trick of
the heart', Monroe Stahr's aristocratic gift of command. All money
was good for was to allow these powers to be exercised.

Apart from anxiety about money, which was terrible to Fitzgerald,
they both soon began to find their roles a strain. Zelda was much too
proud to admit her difficulty, even if there had been an alternative role
that she could endure, but she was finding it difficult to maintain her
pose of confident hedonism and daring without the moral support of
Montgomery and home. Fitzgerald, much of the time, felt lost and
confused. In May 1921 they decided to retire to Westport, Connecticut,
to find peace and quiet, but the parties went right on. 'Parties',
Fitzgerald said, 'are a form of suicide.' Nevertheless, by autumn they
were back in New York, having found Westport insupportably
dreary.

In the spring Zelda discovered she was pregnant and Fitzgerald rushed *The Beautiful and Damned* to completion so that they could take a quick trip abroad that summer. They found Europe 'a bore and a disappointment', and they hurried home to spend the summer in St Paul waiting for their child to arrive. The baby, a daughter, was born on 26 October. Zelda found her a burden; she also hated the terrible cold of St Paul's winter. 'This damned place', she wrote a friend, 'is 18 below zero and I go around thanking God that, anatomically and proverbially speaking, I am safe from the awful fate of the monkey.'

On 3 March 1922 *The Beautiful and Damned* was published. It was a serious book, too serious perhaps, for one of its major defects is a visible conflict between Fitzgerald's direct, natural feelings and the

(*Above*) Zelda in a hotel bedroom during the Fitzgeralds' trip abroad in 1921. The picture gives a fair impression of Zelda's housekeeping habits.

(*Below*) the Fitzgeralds in Venice. The inscription at the right, in Zelda's hand, is on the back of the photograph.

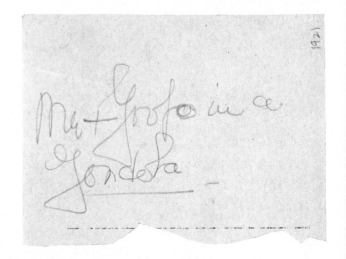

(*Right*) *Vanity Fair*'s choice of the leading young writers in February 1922.

GILBERT SELDES
Formerly American correspondent of the *Echo de Paris*, and now managing editor of The Dial; author of some of the most brilliant critical articles which have appeared in that magazine

JOHN PEALE BISHOP
Princeton, 1917. Author of "Green Fruit," a thin volume of verses; collaborator with Edmund Wilson Jr. on "The Undertaker's Garland"; a contributor of book reviews and other articles to Vanity Fair

NICKOLAS MURAY

NICKOLAS MURAY

DONALD OGDEN STEWART
Mr. Stewart has already received wide recognition on account of his humorous essays and his amusing "Parody Outline of History"

JOHN V. A. WEAVER
Literary editor of the Brooklyn Daily Eagle; author of "In American," a widely read volume of verse in the American language

PIRIE MACDONALD

PIRIE MACDONALD

JOHN DOS PASSOS
A graduate of Harvard, 1918; author of "Three Soldiers," probably the most substantial work yet produced by the younger generation

JOHN FARRAR
Mr. Farrar is now editor of The Bookman and has published two volumes of verse, "Forgotten Shrines" and "Songs for Parents"

WHITE STUDIOS

STEPHEN VINCENT BENET
At the age of twenty-four Mr. Benét has published three books of poems of which the latest, "Heavens and Earth", divided the prize of the Poetry Society, a successful novel "The Beginning of Wisdom" and has completed a second novel "Young People's Pride"

EDMUND WILSON, JR.
A contributor of brilliant and informed critical essays to The New Republic and other periodicals; one of the authors of "The Undertaker's Garland"

F. SCOTT FITZGERALD
Who found immediate fame on the publication of "This Side of Paradise", written at the age of twenty-two; his second novel is "The Beautiful and Damned"

The New Generation in Literature
A Group of Young Writers Who Have Come Upon Old Age While Still in Their Twenties

fashionable attitudes he had been painstakingly learning from the intellectual world of his time. He tried hard to absorb the sentimental pessimism he discovered among approved intellectuals like George Jean Nathan and H. L. Mencken, and to produce what the dust-jacket of the novel – almost certainly at his behest – called 'a devastating satire [on] . . . the wealthy, floating population which throngs the restaurants, cabarets, theaters, and hotels of our great cities.' This fashionable satire was at odds with the book's other subject, Fitzgerald's characteristic effort to search out the meaning of the life he and Zelda had been leading. This part of the book is often very moving. But Fitzgerald, as one reviewer put it, 'has trusted . . . his doctrine rather more than his gusto'. Even when he did trust his gusto and told the story of Gloria and Anthony straight, he was not able to make them what he wanted to, two gifted and beautiful people who refused to

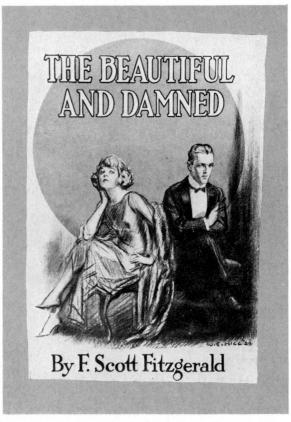

(*Left*) Zelda at White Bear Lake in the summer of 1922.

(*Above*) W. E. Hill's dust jacket for *The Beautiful and Damned*. 'The girl is excellent of course,' Fitzgerald wrote Perkins, ' – it looks somewhat like Zelda but the man, I suspect, is a sort of debauched edition of me. . . .'

compromise with an ugly and vulgar world, and then found they were not strong enough to go it alone. What he plainly wanted them to be was people, capable of using with superior grace and intelligence the opportunities that wealth provides, who were deprived of the opportunity to do so by stupid and absurd prejudice. What he made them was people who craved luxury and the constant stimulation that turns rapidly into dissipation. They are pitiful and silly, rather than beautiful and damned. He could make readers feel what he felt about the life he and Zelda had been living, but not until he wrote *The Great Gatsby* would he be able to define convincingly the reasons for their defeat.

The sales of *The Beautiful and Damned* were, at least by ordinary standards, good; within its first year it sold slightly more than 40,000 copies. This was not good enough for Fitzgerald, however, who was, by publication day, $5600 in debt to Scribner's for advances. This inability, as he conceived it, to make a living out of his writing was beginning to depress him, but the consequences were, at least for the moment, muted by the sale of *This Side of Paradise* to the movies for the then considerable sum of $10,000. In June they moved out to the Yacht Club at White Bear Lake to spare Zelda domestic duties and to be near the summer parties. They were making a defiant gesture in

Zelda with Scottie, taken at the same time as the photograph on the opposite page.

Zelda and Fitzgerald on the dock at White Bear Lake, summer 1922.

A 1922 Rolls-Royce. In that year the Fitzgeralds owned a second-hand Rolls-Royce in which they drove back and forth between Great Neck and New York.

support of the Twenties' conception of the Good Life they held to with such naive literalness.

> I should think [Zelda wrote] that fully airing the desire for unadulterated gaiety, for romance that she knows will not last, and for dramatizing herself would make [a woman] more inclined to favor the 'back to the fireside' movement than if she were repressed until age gives her these rights that only youth has the right to give. I refer to the right to experiment with herself as a transient, poignant figure who will be dead tomorrow.

As far as possible – and with them that was quite far – they were going to 'air the desire for unadulterated gaiety' and then, duly disillusioned, settle into old age – or commit suicide: Fitzgerald's first deadline for suicide was thirty; he gradually advanced the date until – sadly enough, for he never reached it – he settled on fifty.

In October they decided to move back to New York. They rented a house in Great Neck and bought a second-hand Rolls-Royce (their cars were always glamorous but second-hand). Their regular late-night trip back to Great Neck from a party at the Palais Royal, the Plantation, the Rendezvous, or the Club Gallant, was always an odyssey; it was usual for their Japanese man to find them asleep on the lawn the next morning. When they were not in New York, their friends were in Great Neck. 'It became', Fitzgerald said, 'a habit with many world-weary New Yorkers to pass their week-ends at the Fitzgerald house in the country.' 'I wonder', Hemingway wrote him when they became friends shortly after this, 'what your idea of heaven would be – A beautiful vacuum filled with wealthy monogamists all powerful and members of the best families all drinking themselves to death.'

They lived this way for a year. With considerable effort Fitzgerald produced enough work for the magazines to keep them going in the style they were accustomed to, a style that he once said cost considerably

(*Above*) Paul Whiteman and his Band, the most famous dance band of the Twenties. They frequently played at the Palais Royal, one of New York's most popular night clubs.

(*Left*) cover of *The Smart Set* for June 1922, containing 'The Diamond as Big as the Ritz'.

This fancy study of Zelda made in the early Twenties might well have been the work of Chester McKee, the artistic photographer of *The Great Gatsby*. Nevertheless it is an excellent likeness.

An illustration for 'The Millionaire's Girl', published in *The Saturday Evening Post*, 17 May 1930, and accidentally ascribed to Fitzgerald though actually written by Zelda, perhaps as an unconscious commentary on the Fitzgeralds' life in the Twenties.

more than the $36,000 a year he made. Then in October Sam Harris put into rehearsal a play called *The Vegetable* that Fitzgerald had been writing off and on for a couple of years. A fantasy-satire on American society with a Mencken message, it was destined – Fitzgerald had gradually convinced himself – to make him a fortune. In November it opened in Atlantic City and was a catastrophic flop. When they got home to Great Neck, Fitzgerald found himself – as usual to his astonishment and dismay – $5000 in debt. He did the only thing he knew how to do; he went on the wagon, retired to a large unfinished room over his garage, and wrote himself out of the jam. Between November and April he produced eleven stories and earned over $17,000. To do that he overworked seriously: he claimed it took him six months to get over the resulting insomnia and a hacking cough. Moreover, he hated the work itself: 'It was all trash,' he said (though it wasn't), 'and it nearly broke my heart as well as my iron constitution.'

It was in Great Neck that they got to know Ring Lardner for whom Fitzgerald conceived a great admiration. Lardner was, he thought, 'proud, shy, solemn, shrewd, polite, brave, kind, merciful, honorable. . . . Under any conditions a noble dignity flowed from him. . . .' That anyone with these qualities and Lardner's undoubted gifts should, out of some inexplicable despair, quietly go about destroying himself both fascinated and frightened Fitzgerald. He was haunted by the idea that, in spite of his hatred of self-destruction, he too might find himself helplessly destroying himself; and he knew that, with all his Irish

A Covarrubias caricature of Ring Lardner published in *Vanity Fair*, July 1925. Lardner was Fitzgerald's closest friend in the Great Neck days.

A photograph of Ring Lardner and his family in Great Neck published in *Vanity Fair*, March 1923.

ebullience, he would never achieve Lardner's dignity and restraint, deeply as he admired them. Much later, in *Tender Is the Night*, Fitzgerald gave Abe North what he understood of Lardner's attitude; and all through *Tender Is the Night* there runs a subdued parallel between Abe North and Dick Diver, whose decline is Fitzgerald's own.

After his winter's burst of money-making, Fitzgerald found himself some $7000 ahead. He and Zelda decided that they could not live reasonably at Great Neck but could do so in Europe, where, everyone told them, it was very cheap. 'We were going to the Old World to find a new rhythm for our lives,' Fitzgerald wrote, 'with a true conviction that we had left our old selves behind forever. . . .' After a characteristically confused trip they wound up at St Raphaël. For a while novelty kept them happy and Fitzgerald grew optimistic, imagining that he could finish his novel in a month and come triumphantly home in the autumn. Then in July there was trouble.

Zelda and a handsome French aviator named Edouard Josanne fell very much in love. When Fitzgerald discovered what had happened, he asserted himself violently and undignifiedly; Josanne departed and Zelda yielded quietly, as she always did, to Fitzgerald's assertion of authority in a crisis. She had transferred to Fitzgerald – perhaps more out of necessity than belief in him – that final authority she had once given her father; however much she might resent and resist their dominance in ordinary circumstances, she accepted it with the stoicism of a deep need for some kind of authority in crises like this. Of the episode in Zelda's *Save Me the Waltz* that is based on her affair with Josanne, her heroine says, 'What was the use of keeping [the photograph her lover had left her]? . . . There wasn't a way to hold on to the summer. . . . Whatever it was she wanted from [him], [he] took

A sample of the galley proofs of *The Great Gatsby*, from the Plaza Hotel scene. This is a typical example of the extensive revisions Fitzgerald made right up to the last moment.

with him. . . . You took what you wanted from life, if you could get it, and you did without the rest.' Both the courage and the hopelessness of that are typical of Zelda.

The effect of this episode on Fitzgerald was very great. Love was for him, as it was for Jay Gatsby, an incarnation; to the woman of his choice he committed all his dreams of a great life. This was the largest investment of emotional capital he would ever make. Sexual matters were so serious to Fitzgerald because they were final, an irreversible physical expression of the elaborate structure of sentiment that he built around the girl he loved. 'That September 1924,' he wrote in his Notebooks long after, 'I knew something had happened that could never be repaired.'

Oddly enough, this crisis did not slow his work down; in August he had gone on the wagon and begun to make real progress with his novel. Early in November he sent it off, and, to relax, they decided to spend the winter in Rome. It was a bad time. They were drinking heavily again and often quarreled bitterly. They hated Rome; it was cold; they were constantly being pushed aside by headwaiters to make way for Roman aristocrats. The climax came when, in drunken exasperation, Fitzgerald got in a fight with a taxi driver in the course of which he inadvertently slugged a plain-clothes man. Before Zelda could bribe enough people to get him out of jail he had been badly beaten up. This episode haunted Fitzgerald; it seemed to him clear evidence of his deterioration, and he later used it as the climactic episode of Dick Diver's decline. He and Zelda spent the winter in Capri, where they were both ill. Just as *Gatsby* was being published – the official date was 10 April – they decided to drive from Marseilles to Paris. Characteristically their car broke down in Lyons and they went the rest of the way by train (thus providing the occasion for Fitzgerald's trip back to Lyons with Hemingway that is described in *A Moveable Feast*).

The Great Gatsby was an amazing leap forward for Fitzgerald. He had found a hero who would allow him to express far more of his deepest feelings about experience than his earlier heroes had and – much more important, for Fitzgerald's grasp of mood and feeling had always been great – he had found a form that would allow him to order these feelings. None of this was perhaps very self-conscious. He more or less stumbled on the fashionable Long Island bootlegger, Max Von Guerlach, who gave him his idea for Gatsby. He had been reading Conrad, from whom he evidently derived the first-person narration of the novel. He seems to have found his dazzling imagery almost any-where. Doctor T. J. Eckleburg's billboard, for example, was the result of Max Perkins's showing him the design for a dust-jacket just before he and Zelda sailed for the Riviera. It was a very bad picture calculated to suggest – by two enormous eyes – Daisy brooding over an amusement-park version of New York (it was eventually in fact

For Carmel Myers
    from her Corrupter
        F Scott Fitzgerald
"Don't cry, little girl,
maybe someday someon
will come along who'll
make you a dishonest
woman"
        Los Angeles.

(*Above*) Carmel Myers in *Ben Hur*, which was made in Rome in the winter of 1924–25 when the Fitzgeralds were living there; they saw a good deal of the company. Sometime later Fitzgerald wrote the inscription on the left for Carmel Myers in a copy of *The Great Gatsby*.

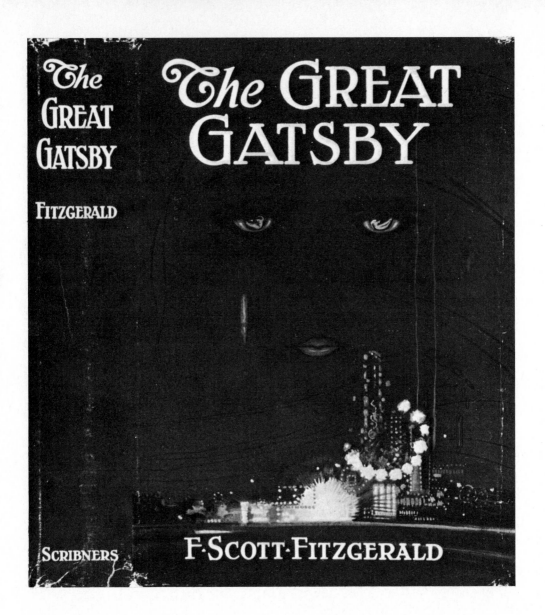

The dust jacket of *The Great Gatsby*. 'Well, go and see an amusement park,' says Father Schwartz in 'Absolution'. '. . . You'll see a big wheel made of lights turning in the air, and . . . a band playing some-where, and a smell of peanuts – and everything will twinkle . . . but don't get up close, because if you do you'll only feel the heat and the sweat and the life.'

used for the dust-jacket). After he got to the Riviera, Fitzgerald wrote Perkins: 'For Christ's sake don't give anyone that jacket you're saving for me. I've written it into the book.'

Fitzgerald's use of a narrator allowed him to separate the two sides of his nature that in his earlier novels had so often bumbled confusingly into one another, the middle-western Trimalchio and the cultivated, spoiled priest, who was at once appalled by Trimalchio's vulgarity and aware of the idealism he was trying to express by means of it. Those terrible shirts with 'stripes and scrolls and plaids in coral and apple green and lavender and faint orange, with monograms of Indian blue'

70

A Hispano Suiza specially designed for Edsel Ford, from a photograph in *Vanity Fair*, April 1923. Fitzgerald must have had in mind one very like this when he described Jay Gatsby's car.

that Gatsby has so painstakingly imported from England to make him worthy of Daisy – no wonder, when he pours them out on the table before her, she suddenly bows her head and weeps. These are the things Nick Carroway can show us.

As a Yale man Nick is fully prepared to respond to the beauty and charm of the Buchanans' life and to disapprove of Gatsby's pink rag of a suit, his blindingly loud car, his recently purchased ancestral mansion. At the same time he is uncomfortable with the 'basic insincerity' that underlies all Daisy's grace and charm, and is appealed to by some indefinable sincerity in Gatsby. By the end he sees clearly that Tom and Daisy, who spent their lives drifting 'here and there unrestfully wherever people played polo and were rich together,' 'were careless people . . . [who] smashed up things and creatures and then retreated back into their money or their vast carelessness, or whatever it was that kept them together, and let other people clean up the mess they had made. . . .' He finally came to recognize – as he said to Gatsby when he left him for the last time – that 'they're a rotten crowd. You're worth the whole damn bunch put together.' The 'incorruptible dream' beneath the superficial corruption and bad taste of Gatsby's life was of inestimable value, a 'heightened sensitivity to the promises of life' that purified everything he did. 'No,' Nick says, ' – Gatsby turned out all right at the end; it is what preyed on Gatsby, what foul dust floated in the wake of his dreams' that was terrible.

Back in Paris, Fitzgerald had to face a new disappointment over the sales of *Gatsby*, which were about 20,000 copies, barely enough to cover the advance. He now began to talk about not going on as a novelist unless novel-writing 'will support me with no more intervals of trash'. But in fact it had; during the first five years of his career Fitzgerald's income had been around $25,000 a year. His conviction that the great life required the mobility and grace of the rich forced him to try to live like a rich man, something that – given his inability to handle money – was very expensive indeed.

He later called that summer of 1925 one of '1000 parties and no work'. It was, perhaps, the turning point of his life, for it was during that summer that the gap between the way he behaved and the way he afterwards thought of himself as having behaved became serious, so that in effect he began to break one of the two basic rules of his life, that

(*Above*) the Fitzgeralds in their Paris apartment in the rue de Tilsitt in 1925.

(*Right*) the Dome, a favorite café of expatriate writers in the mid-Twenties, about 1925.

'*I do not lie to myself.*' In *A Moveable Feast* Hemingway describes a truly horrible transformation that came over Fitzgerald one night that summer when he was drinking at the Dingo, an episode that Fitzgerald later described as drinking 'a few glasses of wine'. Slowly the life that Zelda had so innocently and confidently described as a search for 'unadulterated gaiety' was turning into a terrible and apparently inescapable nightmare. Like Father Schwartz, the mad priest of 'Absolution', who had found the distant prospect of the world's fair so enchanting, they were discovering that if you got up close, you 'only feel the heat and the sweat and the life'.

La Place Nationale, Antibes. The
Fitzgeralds were in Antibes during
1925.

That fall they went to Antibes for a month. There was no one there,
Fitzgerald reported, except 'the Valentinos, the Murphys, Mistinguett,
Rex Ingram, Dos Passos, Alice Terry, the MacLeishes, Charles
Brackett, Maud Kahn, Esther Murphy, Marguerite Namara, E.
Phillips Oppenheim, Mannes the violinist, Floyd Dell, Max and
Crystal Eastman, ex-Premier Orlando, Etienne de Baumont – just a
real place to rough it and escape from all the world. But we had a
great time.' This was the Antibes where Gerald and Sara Murphy
were making an astonishing success of the very life the Fitzgeralds had
dreamed of living, that revenge on everything drab and cruel and
destructive in the world that consisted in living well. That they did it
by intense self-discipline and very firm authority over the friends who
shared their life was something the Fitzgeralds were incapable by this
time of recognizing. They had reached a stage that was difficult for

74

(*Above right*) Gerald and Sara Murphy with
Archibald and Ada MacLeish. This photograph
was taken in Vienna sometime in the 1920s.

(*Right*) Rudolph Valentino, who was also at
Antibes the summer of 1925.

(*Above*) the Villa America, the Murphys' place at Antibes. This terrace was the model for the Divers' in *Tender Is the Night* and was also the scene of Philip Barry's play, *Hotel Universe*.

(*Right*) Gerald and Sara Murphy on the beach at Antibes. *Tender Is the Night* is dedicated 'To Gerald and Sara Many Fêtes'. Dick Diver, the hero of *Tender Is the Night*, is modeled on Gerald Murphy, and the novel's opening scene takes place on this beach.

Ernest Hemingway in the mid-Twenties when Fitzgerald was hard at work getting him started as a novelist and making sure Max Perkins published *The Sun Also Rises*.

others as well as themselves, a stage at which they required a kind of excitement no ordered life could provide. When they were left out of a party, they would stand outside the Murphys' garden and throw garbage over the wall; one night, for no reason at all, Fitzgerald suddenly kicked out of the hands of an old lady in Nice her small tray of paper cornucopias of nuts and candies. Another, when they encountered Isadora Duncan at a small inn and it became clear she had selected Fitzgerald as her partner for the night, Zelda suddenly rose and threw herself down a long flight of steps. On yet another, when they had been fighting, she lay down in front of the car and told Fitzgerald to go ahead and run over her, as he was apparently prepared to do if friends had not stopped him.

It was during this summer of 1924 at Antibes that Fitzgerald started to work on the first version of the novel that would eventually become *Tender Is the Night*. But he made little progress with it. There were many parties in Paris that fall and winter, and more in London. By now, Fitzgerald was quarreling with everybody, even the Murphys. But it was during the following winter, too, that he took up with all his characteristic generosity and enthusiasm the cause of Hemingway, whom he had just met. He worked on Perkins to take Hemingway on, wrote an article plugging him, and buttonholed fellow writers. 'It simply had not occurred to him', Glenway Wescott remarked with amusement, 'that unfriendliness or pettiness on my part might inhibit my enthusiasm about the art of a new colleague and rival.' After a series of incredibly complicated maneuvers, Hemingway was finally safely installed at Scribner's and Fitzgerald then began to fuss over Hemingway's new novel, *The Sun Also Rises*. In the spring, Hemingway came down to visit the Fitzgeralds at Juan-les-Pins with the carbon of the novel, having already sent the ribbon copy to Scribner's. Fitzgerald persuaded him to 'cut the Sun to start with Cohn – cut all that first part', and give the novel the form in which it was finally printed.

Again, the Fitzgeralds spent their summer on the Riviera. There were more of the Murphys' fine parties and many practical jokes, such as the elaborate scheme Fitzgerald and Charles McArthur concocted for sawing a waiter in two – with a musical saw to 'eliminate any sordidness'; they gave it up when Zelda told them they would find nothing inside but old menus, tips, pencil stubs, and broken china. Zelda's symbolic gestures were grimmer than that. At a farewell party that fall for Alexander Woollcott and 'Chato' Elizaga, after a large number of toasts, she got up and said 'I have been so touched by all these kind words. But what are words? Nobody has offered our departing heroes any gifts to take with them. I'll start off,' and she stepped out

(*Below left*) Lois Moran, the actress, in the Twenties. Fitzgerald met her in Hollywood in 1927 and modeled Rosemary Hoyt of *Tender Is the Night* on her. (*Below right*) John Barrymore in a photograph made for *Vanity Fair*, January 1920. Barrymore was another Hollywood friend and party companion of the Fitzgeralds.

of her black lace panties and threw them to Woollcott and Elizaga. By this time Fitzgerald was getting almost no work done. His novel was at a standstill and he would not publish a single story between February 1926 and June 1927. At the end of 1925 they decided to go back to America. It was an unhappy return. Fitzgerald felt himself to be a man whose deterioration, like Dick Diver's, had gone a lot further than was apparent. 'At first,' as Dick says, 'it didn't show. The manner remains intact for some time after the morale cracks.'

Fitzgerald on the set in Hollywood with Richard Barthelmess in 1927.

They came back to America determined to settle down to the orderly life; Fitzgerald was going to get a lot of work done. Almost immediately, however, there was an offer from United Artists to come to Hollywood and do a script for 'one of the hectic flapper comedies, in which Constance Talmadge had specialized for years'. They were made much of in Hollywood, lunching at Pickfair and going on many parties with Lillian Gish and Lois Moran, John Barrymore and Richard Barthelmess. Fitzgerald was fascinated by Lois Moran. He

Constance Talmadge in the Twenties. Fitzgerald went to Hollywood in 1927 specifically to write for her 'one of the hectic flapper comedies, in which [she] had specialized for years'. His script, called *Lipstick*, was rejected.

was thirty and hated it, and she was twenty; her youth, her beauty, her admiration enchanted him. Nearly a decade later, when she came to see him in Baltimore, the occasion seemed to him so moving that he planned a story around it. Eventually he put many of his feelings about her into his portrait of Rosemary Hoyt in *Tender Is the Night*.

But their life in Hollywood was by no means the settled one they had planned to live; rather, like the old life in Paris, it turned into an almost continuous party to which they contributed more and more frantic jokes. One day at Carmel Myers', Fitzgerald collected watches and jewelry from the guests and then boiled them in a couple of cans of tomato soup. Once very late at night, at John Monk Saunders', Zelda offered to perform an operation for Saunders with the library shears that would, she assured him, greatly simplify his life. When Fitzgerald completed his script for Constance Talmadge it was rejected. They piled all the furniture in the middle of their room at the Ambassador, put their unpaid bills on top of the pile, and departed.

Once more they attempted to settle down. They rented a beautiful old Greek-Revival house near Wilmington, Delaware, that was, Zelda said, 'to bring us a judicious tranquility'. During the summer of 1927 Fitzgerald got some serious work done on his novel, the first for a long time. But they were both nervously on edge and their personal relations were slowly deteriorating into what Fitzgerald later called an 'organized cat and dog fight'. Gradually they drifted back into the old life of restlessness and parties. In February, Fitzgerald answered an inquiry from Max Perkins by saying, 'novel not yet finished. Christ I wish it were!' Then they decided to go to Paris for the summer of 1928. Zelda had, abruptly (at the age of twenty-eight), decided to become a ballet dancer, an ambition that went back to her girlhood. She began to work at it with an intensity that one of their friends described, with more literal accuracy than he knew, as like the dancing madness of the Middle Ages. There is something desperate and pitiful about this sudden commitment; behind it must have lain some feeling that there was no shelter at all left for her in that exquisite and superior world she and Fitzgerald had set out to build together with such confidence scarcely ten years before.

Zelda in ballet costume at Ellerslie, outside Wilmington, probably in the summer of 1929, when they gave up Ellerslie, sent their possessions to Zelda's family in Montgomery, and went to Paris, where Zelda wanted to train as a dancer.

The Fitzgeralds arriving at a performance of
Dinner at Eight in Baltimore in 1932.

They reached Paris in a haze of alcohol, without reservations or
plans. They were quarreling bitterly now; Fitzgerald clearly resented
the successful if neurotic discipline with which Zelda concentrated on
her dancing while he was so evidently wasting his time in dissipation.
Twice that summer he ended up in jail. 'It is', as Zelda later said, 'the
loose-ends with which men hang themselves.' The summer came to a
climax in a violent, destructive quarrel in which Zelda taunted

Fitzgerald with his sexual inadequacy, accused him of being a homo-sexual, and hinted that she herself preferred women. In September they came back to Wilmington 'in a blaze of work & liquor', as Fitzgerald put it. His novel was far from finished; he was having a harder and harder time producing the short stories on which they depended for an income; they were broke, though their income that year was close to $30,000. That winter in Wilmington Fitzgerald continued to roam, restless and drunk, and to land up in jail, and Zelda went on – in Fitzgerald's words – 'dancing and sweating'. In the spring of 1928 they gave up on Wilmington and returned once more to Paris, where, despite Fitzgerald's efforts to convince himself – or at least Perkins – that he would be able to finish his novel by the fall, things became, if anything, worse.

My latest tendency [Fitzgerald wrote, with his terrible objectivity] is to collapse about 11:00 and, with tears flowing from my eyes or the gin rising to their level and leaking over, tell interested friends and acquaintances that I haven't a friend in the world and likewise care for nobody, generally including Zelda, and often implying current company – after which the current company tend to become less current and I wake up in strange [places] . . . when drunk I make them pay and pay and pay.

Zelda was now beginning to hope for engagements as a dancer and she did get one or two small ones, but she was dreaming of an offer from Diaghilev. None came, and, 'to forget bad times', they went on a sight-seeing trip to Algiers in February. Fitzgerald later used the trip for a story, which is a preliminary study for Dick and Nicole Diver, and a judgment of their own lives. The story describes an attractive

The Depression.

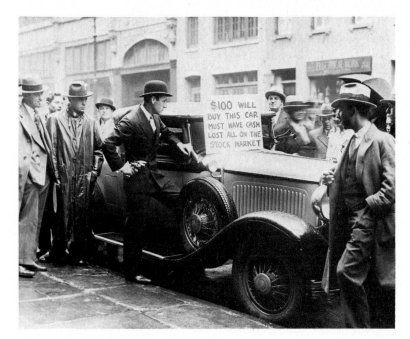

83

(*Above left*) Zelda as she appeared just before her breakdown, probably in 1929 (compare the photograph on p. 81 taken at the same time). (*Above right*) This snapshot was taken in 1931 when, for the first time since she had broken down in April 1930, Zelda was well enough to leave the sanitarium. In the family photograph album it is entitled 'Recovered'.

young couple who get mixed up with 'a crowd of drunks' in Europe and gradually deteriorate until, seeing himself in a bar mirror, the hero recognizes 'the kind of face that needs half a dozen drinks really to open the eyes and stiffen the mouth up to normal'; and the heroine says in bewilderment, 'It's just that we don't understand what's the matter. Why did we lose peace and love and health, one after the other? If we knew, if there was anybody to tell us, I believe we could try. I'd try so hard.' They had set out with innocently arrogant self-confidence to find the good life where their stuffy elders had told them life was dangerous, in beautiful 'civilized' places where 'interesting' people lived cultured lives and somehow managed to be serious artists without ceasing to practice the ritual of Paris parties and Riviera beaches. And they had ended in emotional bankruptcy.

When they got back from Algiers Zelda – fighting off knowledge of failure – worked harder than ever, and grew tenser and tenser, until in April she had a serious breakdown. It was Fitzgerald's nature to feel deeply the suffering of someone he loved, and something of what Zelda now suffered and his feelings about her is in the description of Doctor Diver's treatment of his anonymous patient who, suffering

84

A self-portrait of Zelda some time in the early 1940s.

from eczema like a person 'imprisoned in the Iron Maiden', yet remained 'coherent, even brilliant, within the limits of her special hallucinations'. To intensify his sympathy and remorse, Fitzgerald had his knowledge of how much he had contributed to Zelda's collapse, however inevitable – as the doctors all assured him was the case – it had been. He knew he had often been unsympathetic about her dancing and her unhappiness and it must have sounded like the voice of his own conscience when the doctors told him that 'one of the things that haunted her in her delirium' was his drinking. He put all these feelings about his treatment of Zelda into 'Babylon Revisited'.

It was not until the fall of 1931 that she grew well enough for them to leave Switzerland and go home to Montgomery. Hardly had they arrived than Fitzgerald got an invitation to go to Hollywood to do a script of Katherine Brush's *Red-Headed Woman* for Metro-Goldwyn-Mayer. Bored by the quiet life and ready as always to respond to the excitement of the movies, he accepted eagerly. He had a good time in Hollywood and provided himself with the material for a fine story, 'Crazy Sunday'. But the script was a failure; moreover, while he was away, Judge Sayre died. Zelda reacted badly to his death and, in

A society-page photograph of Zelda
and Scottie from the *Baltimore Sun* in
the early 1930s.

January, broke down again completely. It was a stunning blow: they
now knew enough about schizophrenia to be aware that, with each
breakdown, a final recovery was less likely. Zelda went to the
Phipps Clinic in Baltimore. During her first month and a half
there she wrote her novel, *Save Me the Waltz*. When it was finished
she sent it straight to Perkins, a gesture at once violently anti-Fitzgerald
and pathetic, since even she must have known she could not circum-
vent Fitzgerald by turning to Perkins. Between him and Fitzgerald,
she was eventually persuaded to tone down its central section which
was a violent attack on Fitzgerald. She did not improve, and –
anticipating a long struggle – Fitzgerald moved himself and his
daughter to a rambling Victorian house on the Bayard Turnbull

estate at Rodgers Forge, next door to Phipps Clinic. By June, Zelda was well enough to be there a good deal of the time.

Their life at La Paix – as their house was called ('La Paix,' Fitzgerald said; 'my God!') – was an ironic change from the one they had committed themselves to with such confidence scarcely a decade earlier. In 1933 Fitzgerald said they had dined out exactly four times in two years. They were now engaged in a last-ditch battle against Zelda's schizophrenia and Fitzgerald's alcoholism, and what is more important, they knew it. 'No one', as a close friend of those days said, 'could watch that struggle and not be convinced of the reality of [Fitzgerald's] concern and suffering.' It was the last, dogged assertion of his impulse to come up off the floor fighting after a terrible blow.

Fitzgerald in his study at La Paix, where most of *Tender Is the Night* was written. Fitzgerald always remembered sitting at this desk, 'Alone in the privacy of my faded blue room with my sick cat, the bare February branches waving at the window, an ironic paperweight that says business is good . . . .' The paperweight, a miniature parking sign, is on the left side of the desk. There is a picture of it on p. 115.

(*Left*) La Paix, the Victorian house on the Bayard Turnbull property in Towson, Maryland, which Fitzgerald rented while Zelda was at the Phipps Clinic during 1932 and 1933. (*Below*) in June 1933, Zelda tried to burn some old clothes in an unused upstairs fireplace in La Paix and set the house afire. This is the scene on the lawn the next morning after the fire had been put out.

To a friend who urged them to join in the old revelry, he wrote, '. . . you insist on a world which we will willingly let die, in which Zelda can't live, which damned near ruined us both. . . .' They had, he thought, come a long way in their struggle to save themselves but they were far from safe yet. Zelda continued to show serious signs of instability – flashes of violence and rashness that seemed to come from nowhere. With the nervous tension of his work – he was struggling desperately now to finish *Tender Is the Night* – and his drinking, Fitzgerald was not the easiest person to live with, especially as one of the things that disturbed Zelda most was the old, unresolved rivalry between them. She was no doubt often a genuine problem for Fitzgerald, for in what she wrote she often used material from their lives that he had been counting on for his work – work that, with some justice, he thought of as more important than hers, especially financially, a matter of some seriousness since their financial situation had greatly deteriorated. Their income had fallen by half in 1932, at a time when Fitzgerald's capacity to turn out saleable short stories was decreasing; he now insisted that alcohol was necessary to him if he were to write at all, though he was more easily incapacitated by it than most people. In addition it made him irritable and insensitive, so that he was often unkind to Zelda about aspects of her work that meant a good deal to her and did not affect his work at all.

Then in January 1934, Zelda broke down badly once more; by May she was in a catatonic state. For the next six years, except for brief vacations, she was confined to various hospitals. 'I left my capacity for hoping,' Fitzgerald said, 'on the little roads that led to Zelda's sanitarium.' Gradually, as time passed, their lives grew apart and their letters became more and more sadly impersonal. But the tragedy, with all its loss and remembrance, was always there for them both, something almost too terrible to contemplate. Sometime shortly before Fitzgerald died, Zelda wrote him,

Dearest and always Dearest Scott:
    I am sorry too that there should be nothing to greet you but an empty shell. . . .
    I want you to be happy – if there were any justice you would be happy – maybe you will be anyway.
    Oh, Do-Do-Do –
    I love you anyway – even if there isn't any me or any love or even any life –
    I love you.

It is not easy even for an outsider to contemplate that reality steadily.

During this time of Zelda's third and, in effect, final breakdown Fitzgerald was struggling with the proofs of *Tender Is the Night*, which was finally published on 12 April 1934. It was not a success. By this time Fitzgerald's characteristic material – well-to-do and ostensibly idle people living on the Riviera – was anathema to most

(*Left*) Zelda painting at La Paix. (*Above*) Fitzgerald as fisherman in the early Thirties.

reviewers, who were busy promoting the proletarian novel. They judged the book 'a rather irritating type of chic', with a 'clever and brilliant surface but . . . not wise and mature'. Fitzgerald knew the book had faults. He was aware that, writing it 'on stimulant', as he put it, he had been unable to hold the whole novel in his mind at once, so that the selection and emphasis of the book are sometimes imperfect. He was worried about the complexity of its point of view, especially the long opening section that focuses attention on Rosemary Hoyt. And he knew that, however well he sensed what had gone wrong for

Fitzgerald at 1307 Park Avenue in Baltimore, a house to which they moved when they left La Paix late in 1933. The extent of Fitzgerald's weariness and despair begins to show in pictures like this one.

Two of Edward Shenston's sensitive period decorations for *Tender Is the Night*. The one above shows Rosemary on the beach in the novel's first scene. The one on the left shows her on her bedroom terrace the night before the duel.

Dick Diver, he had not made Dick's character obvious for the reader.

But these defects, real as they are, are insignificant beside the book's richness, its depth and penetration of understanding, its verbal brilliance. In a much more organic way than in *Gatsby*, he makes the fate of his chosen people an image of the fate of Western society. The thing that marks Dick Diver is his possession of a set of manners that are 'a trick of the heart', because they are an expression of his instincts, his feelings for 'honor, courtesy, courage'. It was, perhaps, a weakness in him that, 'wanting to be brave and kind . . . [he] wanted, even more, to be loved', wanted some return for the continual exercise of his powers to give back to the people around him – at least for a moment – 'themselves . . . blurred by the compromises of how many years'. But it was not just a weakness. One thing is very clear about Dick Diver; he illustrates in a classical way Fitzgerald's belief in Emotional Bankruptcy, in the idea that everyone is given just so much

In the fall of 1935, Fitzgerald moved into an apartment in the Cambridge Arms opposite the Johns Hopkins campus – 'The Attic, Cambridge Arms', he used to head his letters. This is the apartment described in *Afternoon of an Author*. From his window he could see this monument to the remote ancestor for whom he was named, Francis Scott Key, the author of 'The Star-Spangled Banner'.

emotional capital and that it is all too easy – if you spend it with a lavish hand without return – to exhaust it. 'I thought of him,' Fitzgerald said of Dick, '. . . as an "homme épuisé", not only an "homme manqué".' In a parallel way he thought of Western Europe as having exhausted itself emotionally in the world war. Standing on one of the battlefields, Dick says of it:

No Europeans will ever do [this kind of thing] again in this generation. . . . This kind of battle was invented by Lewis Carroll and Jules Verne and whoever wrote Undine, and country deacons bowling and marraines in Marseilles and girls seduced in the back lanes of Wurtemburg and Westphalia. . . . There was a century of middle-class love spent here.

The novel ends with Nicole cured of her illness, her character once more solidified into the Warren hardness and assurance to which she was born. Then Dick deliberately breaks her dependence on him and turns her over to Tommy Barban, whose very name suggests what suits her now that she is once more her pure Warren self. Having freed her, he leaves for America, to wander from one to another of the

94

The dust jacket for *Taps at Reveille* (1935), Fitzgerald's last book of short stories.

small, lost towns of upstate New York, as some one or another random undisciplined act destroys his reputation. '. . . his latest note was post‑marked from Hornell, New York, which is some distance from Geneva and a very small town; in any case, he is almost certainly in that section of the country, in one town or another.' Baby Warren speaks the new, loveless world's judgment of his kind of man when Nicole says that for the six years of her illness, Dick had been an almost perfect husband to her, and Baby adds, 'That's what he was educated for.' Fitzgerald's serial title for the novel had been *Doctor Diver's Holiday*.

The failure of a book into which he had put so much of himself, coming on top of his despair over Zelda's situation, was almost too much for Fitzgerald. He struggled through the business of getting ready the volume of short stories – in this instance *Taps at Reveille* – that Scribner's always brought out on the heels of one of his novels and when that job was finished, he fled, not so much perhaps from anything as to some sort of anonymity and privacy where he could try

A contemporary picture of the Grove Park Inn in Asheville, North Carolina, where Fitzgerald lived a good deal of the time in 1936 and 1937 to be close to Zelda, who was in a nearby sanitarium named Highlands.

to face himself. He went first to Tryon and then to Hendersonville, a little resort town about twelve miles from Asheville. Here he struggled to put himself on the wagon. In May he had an attack of tuberculosis; the doctor's reports show that he had had previous mild attacks, and tuberculosis was a disease that had haunted his hypochondriacal imagination since his Princeton days. He prepared himself for a long siege, and then, suddenly, the tuberculosis subsided – 'and [I] cracked like an old plate as soon as I heard the news'.

Fitzgerald duck-shooting near Asheville,
12 January 1936.

He struggled to carry out his obligations to Zelda, making a heroic effort to have her home for that Christmas, and then tried to make some kind of home for his daughter Scottie. But between the severity of the standards he set her as a result of his feelings about how he and Zelda had destroyed themselves and his unreliable behaviour when he was overwrought or drunk, he failed miserably. 'I think of you constantly,' he wrote her the next summer, 'and if I ever prayed it would be that the irritations, exasperations and blow ups of the past winter wouldn't spoil the old confidence we had in each other.' He meant it with all his heart; no one ever loved a daughter better than he loved Scottie. But he was capable of treating her intolerably, and often did in the next few years. His work was now beginning to decline seriously in quality; much of it was rejected and some that was not was taken by editors for old times' sake and never published. 'It grows harder and harder to write now,' he said, 'because there is so much less weather than when I was a boy and practically no men and women at all.' His nerves were less and less reliable. Again and again he would carefully plan some outing to make Zelda happy – he never stopped thinking of her and pitying her – and then, after a few hours with her, would blow up and produce some terrible row. Then one day in the summer of 1936, feeling better than he had for a long time, 'I thought

I would be very smart and do some diving . . . trying to show off for Zelda.' He tore his shoulder muscles so badly his arm was left dangling from the socket. He was laid up for ten weeks, and between the pain, the anxiety of lost work, and the boredom, he began to drink again. An unfortunate newspaper interview on 24 September – his birthday – mercilessly exposed the drunken disorder he now was living in and filled him with fear of its effect on his market.

But this was, in fact, the bottom for him. His shoulder gradually mended and in the fall his mother died, leaving him a small amount of money. With the freedom from pressure this money gave him, he settled down once more to fight his demons. With some sense that he was becoming a different person and could no longer hope to go on writing the kind of thing he had made a living from in the past, he now gave up trying to write for *The Saturday Evening Post* and began a series of autobiographical pieces for *Esquire*. The first of these was a three-part series called *The Crack-Up*. Through the thin disguise of Fitzgerald's still partly fantastic rationalization of what his situation was, this series exposed far more of the truth of his demoralization than he realized and the effect was to destroy – in the way he had so feared his drunken interview would – any immediate chance he might have had for getting the job in Hollywood he had been angling for ever since he had got into serious financial straits in 1934.

There was a strong economic motive for this attempt to get a job in Hollywood. However foolish Fitzgerald's spending of money was, he had never ceased to be horrified by debt; the debts that slowly accumulated during these years of illness and drunkenness were an agony to him. By his own calculations he owed Harold Ober and Max Perkins and Scribner's about $40,000 by the time he went to Hollywood; and they were far from the only people he owed. When, in June 1937, he finally did land a job in Hollywood at $1000 a week, he arranged to deposit his salary with Harold Ober, who was to pay him $400 a month for his own expenditures and apply the rest to his debts. He retained substantially this arrangement until they were all paid off, in spite of the fact that he was often desperate for money.

But money was not his only motive for going to Hollywood. He had always believed in the possibilities of the movies and had always hoped to establish himself in Hollywood. He went there with a sense of excitement about his future that it is difficult to believe was possible for the man who had been so worn and demoralized only six months before. This fresh mood set him planning in his old way to dominate life, to 'fight tooth & nail until, in fact or in effect, I'm alone on the picture. That's the only way I can do my best work. Given a break I can make them double this contract in less than two years.' This was a modest statement of his expectations; what he was really thinking was that he might become a power in the industry, another Irving Thalberg (on whose career he would base the career of Monroe Stahr

A photograph of Fitzgerald taken outside the Algonquin Hotel in New York in
1937 by Carl Van Vechten.

Irving Thalberg, the boy wonder of Hollywood, as he appeared in 1936. Though the private experience of Monroe Stahr, the hero of *The Last Tycoon*, is Fitzgerald's, his Hollywood career is Thalberg's.

of *The Last Tycoon*) or a director who was given absolute authority over his pictures.

To prepare himself for this authority, he worked hard reading and analyzing scripts, having old pictures run off for him. At the beginning he stayed completely sober and for a long time he went on a bust only occasionally. Hope and excitement improved his morale remarkably and he could hardly believe how much better he felt. He even succeeded in taking Zelda on trips in September and again in December

Fitzgerald outside the Garden of Allah, where he lived when he first settled in Hollywood in 1937.

that went off without a hitch. He was not, of course, really a well man, and he soon gave up the modest social life he had attempted. Nor was his morale wholly restored. 'Five years have rolled away from me,' he wrote Perkins, 'and I can't decide exactly who I am, if anyone. . . .' Once, with that irony about himself that was the foundation of his sanity, he wrote himself a postal card that said, 'Dear Scott – How are you? Have been meaning to come in and see you. I have [been] living at the Garden of Allah. Yours Scott Fitzgerald.' In an important sense, Scott Fitzgerald had indeed disappeared. To his old friend Edmund Wilson, he seemed now like a polite stranger; and after that first burst of enthusiasm about Hollywood he was, most of the time, a man simply going through the motions without caring, held together, when he was, by a sense of responsibility alone. Once, after a violent quarrel with Sheilah Graham, he said, 'You don't have to look far for the reason – I was it. . . . I want to die, Sheilah, and in my own way.'

He had met Sheilah Graham almost as soon as he arrived in Holly-wood, at a party at Robert Benchley's. She was a strange girl; she had been born Lily Sheil in London's East End and, by one of those tremendous efforts of will that Fitzgerald had once so deeply believed in, she had worked her way up in the world from chorus girl to newspaper woman to a shaky position in the circle of the Duchess of Devonshire. Beneath the heroic determination that had carried her now to a position as a successful Hollywood gossip columnist there was a girl in many ways almost innocent, certainly inexperienced and

Sheilah Graham, the Hollywood columnist with whom Fitzgerald had a love affair in Hollywood. The character of Kathleen in *The Last Tycoon* is closely modeled on her.

Fitzgerald at the Beverly Hills Tennis Club in the summer of 1937, in a snapshot taken by his daughter, Scottie, who wrote the caption.

Daddy at the Beverly Hills Tennis Club

Fitzgerald and Sheilah on a holiday
in Tijuana, Mexico, early in 1940.

uncertain of herself – badly shaken by the fact that she had never even
heard of most of the things Benchley and his friends talked about.

The best account there will ever be of how Fitzgerald felt about
Sheilah Graham is the story of Stahr and Kathleen in *The Last
Tycoon*. Every step toward his emotional involvement with her is
described with great exactness, only the external circumstances being
changed – and then only when it is necessary to make them fit Stahr's
situation. Fitzgerald certainly loved Sheilah, but he worried –

perhaps justly – about his capacity to meet the demands of a new relation. Nevertheless, so far as his nearly exhausted emotional capital would allow, he gave himself to this one. Sheilah broke an engagement with Lord Donegall that had been made before she met Fitzgerald and they quietly joined forces.

It was an almost miraculous piece of luck for Fitzgerald; it gave him someone to care for and worry over and fight for – something he had not had since the failure of confidence between him and Zelda in the late Twenties – and thus to stay alive. Not all the care and affection in the world could keep him from his frightening bouts of despairing drunkenness, something Sheilah hardly suspected until she had committed herself but faced with great courage when she found out about them. She made a stable world for him and, as much as it was possible for him to do so, made him want to live. After a time he began to go for long spells without drinking and, at the end of his life, remained sober for a stretch of nearly a year.

What seemed to Fitzgerald the longed-for reward of all his efforts to become a movie professional came when, late in 1937, he was given the job of making a script for Erich Remarque's *Three Comrades*. He worked desperately hard over it, only to have the producer take it home for a week-end and rewrite a great part of it. That was the end of his dream of success in the movies. He had other assignments – Joan Crawford's *Infidelity*, which was killed by the censor, and *The Women* and *Madame Curie*; but these were just jobs to him. In

Three Comrades, 1938, starring Robert Young, Robert Taylor, Margaret Sullavan, and Franchot Tone, Fitzgerald thought the script he wrote for this film the best work he did in Hollywood.

A scene from *Winter Carnival*, 1939. Fitzgerald was hired by Walter Wanger to work with Budd Schulberg on the script for this film about Dartmouth, and the two made a disastrously drunken trip to Hanover during which Wanger fired Fitzgerald.

November 1938 Walter Wanger put him on a story about the Dartmouth Winter Carnival with Budd Schulberg. Wanger insisted on their actually going to the Winter Carnival and Fitzgerald made such a drunken spectacle of himself there that Wanger fired him on the spot. He was in the hospital in New York for two weeks before he was well enough to return to Hollywood. As a result of these failures, his contract was not renewed when it ran out and he had to face a new situation.

At first he tried free-lancing and for a time it seemed a possible, though harrowing, way to live. But then the jobs dried up, partly because he was not – with his ill-health and his bouts of drinking – the most reliable writer in Hollywood and partly because his work had not been so successful as to make his name leap to producers' minds. Pathetically enough, he persuaded himself that some of his enemies had put him on a Black List and that he was being systematically excluded from movie work. By March of 1939 he was deeply discouraged and frightened. Scottie was now at Vassar and Zelda in a sanitarium in Asheville; his expenses were heavy and he could not find work. In his anxiety he began to drink again. In April he took Zelda on a trip to Cuba, where in drunken pity he attempted to stop a cockfight and got badly beaten up. When he got back to Hollywood after another session in Doctors Hospital he wrote Perkins that he suspected Harold Ober had 'formed the idea that I am back in the mess of three years ago'. If Ober had, he was perilously close to the truth.

Fitzgerald was now convinced that it was hopeless to try to make a living from the movies and decided to try writing again. He began this new career by getting in a fight with his old and devoted friend

Harold Ober and breaking with him, after almost twenty years. For the rest of his life he dealt directly, and inefficiently, with editors. The twenty-three stories he would write between this time and his death, together with the stories he wrote between *Taps at Reveille* and coming to Hollywood, form with the unfinished *The Last Tycoon* a distin-guishable period in Fitzgerald's career, the fiction of his despair.

By the summer of 1939 he began to get some sort of control of his drinking again and even found a little movie work. But he was still in great financial difficulties, and when, in September, *Collier's* expressed interest in the novel he had been thinking about and he saw a chance to make real money out of it – *Collier's* had offered him $25,000–$30,000 for the serial rights if he would submit fifteen thousand words and an outline they approved – he went to work on it enthusiastically. But he did not have much energy. He could hardly ever work a whole day and much of the time he wrote in bed. In spite of the rapidity with which he could write – he dictated most of the dialogue of *The Last Tycoon* straight off – it took him two months to compose six thousand words, less than half of what *Collier's* had asked for. Nonetheless he rushed it to them and when they said they could not make a decision until they saw more he flew into a rage, broke off negotiations with them, and announced that there were 'no great magazine editors left'. He then went on another despairing and violent drunk during which he quarreled with Sheilah and struck her. It was not until the begin-ning of the new year that he got himself sobered down and made his peace with her, but from then on he remained sober.

Then he got a surprise movie offer that very much excited him. Columbia offered him a small sum (with more to come if the script were accepted) to write a script of 'Babylon Revisited'. He worked six hours a day to complete the first draft – an incredible effort for a man in his condition – and finished the script by the end of June. Then Shirley Temple could not be got to play the lead in the picture and it was shelved. But with the money he had made from this work he was able to return to his novel. His health had grown considerably worse. 'I can't exercise even a little any more,' he told his daughter, 'I'm best off in my room.' He was trying desperately to finish *The Last Tycoon* by December 1940, no doubt because he could calculate that his money would run out by that time. 'I am', he told Zelda, emphasizing the happy part of the truth and ignoring the unhappy, 'deep in my novel, living in it, and it makes me happy.' In November he had what his doctor called a cardiac spasm. He took to his bed and there wrote even harder – now, no doubt, suspicious that not only the money but he himself might run out before the novel was finished. Most of *The Last Tycoon* must have been written between this time and his second heart attack.

Less than half of *The Last Tycoon* exists, even in first draft; the rest we know only in outline, which – if it suggests a rich and fascinating story – is far from proving that Fitzgerald could have realized that story with all its implications about American life that he plainly hoped to make a part of it. Nevertheless what exists is impressive, especially considering that it is only a first draft. The scenes are sharply focused and beautifully clear in purpose, written in that quiet, powerful prose that is characteristic of Fitzgerald's last period. His hero, Monroe Stahr, is deliberately presented as the last of the great paternalistic entrepreneurs. ('You're doing a costume part and you don't know it,' Wylie White says to him, '– the brilliant capitalist of the twenties'.) What finally defeats Stahr is not a failure on his part but the character of modern capitalist enterprise, in which there is no function for the brilliant individual whose talent is for controlling the whole operation by intelligence and understanding. At the center of the 'great dream' with which Fitzgerald said he had lived all his life was the dream of creating and managing some important enterprise. The most recent version of it was his dream of taking command in Hollywood, as Stahr, for a time, does. What fascinated him was responsibility and the authority to fulfill it. 'We cannot', he said, 'just let our worlds crash around us like a lot of dropped trays.'

As we watch Stahr exercising his gift for command to control what is both a great economic enterprise and one of the sources of American mythology, we slowly recognize that *The Last Tycoon* is a political fable. The novel opens with Manny Schwartz committing suicide at Andrew Jackson's Hermitage, not even knowing who Andrew Jackson was but with some vague feeling that the place is appropriate. A little later a European prince, at once impressed and puzzled by Stahr, sees an extra dressed as Lincoln in the studio commissary and thinks, 'This, then . . . was what they all meant to be.' In the last, unfinished part of the book, Stahr was to go to Washington but to be ill and unable – like Manny Schwartz at The Hermitage – to see it clearly.

Whether Fitzgerald could have brought off this complicated novel with its realistic portrait of Hollywood, its intensely felt love story, and its fable of American life is something we can never know. In the middle of December he told Perkins he would be able to complete the first draft by the middle of January. No doubt this was the enthusiasm of a man who knew he was writing well, but he was making real progress. No sooner had he made this prophecy than, on 20 December 1940, he had a second and more severe heart attack. The next day was the doctor's regular one for seeing him, so they did not call him that night. Fitzgerald slept well and the next day occupied himself making notes on the margin of an article about the Princeton football team, on which he had never ceased to fancy himself an authority. Suddenly he started up from his chair, clutched the mantel for a moment, and fell to the floor. In a few moments he was dead.

The back lot of M.G.M. as it appeared about 1935. Here the flood occurs, during which Monroe Stahr of *The Last Tycoon* meets the heroine, Kathleen.

He was laid out in the Wordsworth Room of a Hollywood funeral parlor on 'the wrong side of the tracks'. Few came to see him; but one who did was Dorothy Parker; she stood looking at her old friend for a few minutes and then repeated quietly what 'Owl-Eyes' had said at Gatsby's funeral, 'The poor son of a bitch.' He had asked to be buried with his father in the Catholic cemetery in Rockville, Maryland, but the Church would not allow him there and he was buried in the Rockville Union Cemetery. Not long before he died he had scribbled a few lines of a poem he never finished.

> *Your books were in your desk*
> *I guess and some unfinished*
> *Chaos in your head*
> *Was dumped to nothing by the great janitress*
> *Of destinies.*

On 10 March 1948, Highland Hospital in Asheville burned down, apparently set afire by a pyromaniac. Zelda, who was in a room on the top floor, was trapped there and burned to death; one of her slippers, which was caught under the body and not completely burned up, was all that made it possible to identify her. She was buried beside Fitzgerald and a common headstone stands above their graves.

The tombstone over the common grave of Scott and Zelda Fitzgerald in the Rockville Union Cemetery, Rockville, Maryland.

It is beginning to be clear that the important American writers of the first half of the twentieth century – for all their individual differences – resembled each other in fundamental ways. This resemblance is traceable, ultimately, to the beginnings of the romantic movement, but the romanticism of these writers is strongly marked by characteristics peculiar to American culture, by Puritanism, by the self-dependence and self-confidence of the frontier, by Transcendentalism, and by the particular form of rugged individualism that flourished during the time they were growing up and that is so perfectly represented by the set of directions for self-improvement that James Gatz of Fitzgerald's *The Great Gatsby* set down for himself on the last fly-leaf of a book called *Hopalong Cassidy* on 12 September 1906. Despite the conscious rebellion of their generation against what they believed to be the values of the American past (and quite often were the prejudices of their parents), the belief of these writers that they were redefining the universe for themselves in complete independence is a delusion. The very idea that it was possible to do so was an inherited one.

The convictions on which the attitude more or less common to them all rested are familiar enough. There is first the conviction that what makes anything true is that one has felt it strongly; closely connected with this conviction is the corollary that one can feel strongly only those ideas that one can convince oneself one has thought up entirely independently: the 'sincerity' with which things learned from others is felt is always open to question. The second conviction is that the meaningful link between consciousness and the external world is the association of objects and places with strong personal feelings: it is the intensity of the individual's feelings that gives significance and thus reality to the external world: value dwells in the particular will. This association between personal emotion and place is a psychological phenomenon common to all times, of course, but it takes on an almost theological force in poems like 'Tintern Abbey' or the 'Elegiac Stanzas', to the point where the physical world, though represented with great precision and 'realism', is always saturated with Wordsworth's personal feelings, a symbol and authentication of them. This combination of romantic egotism and realism – sometimes in forms that would have astonished and dismayed Wordsworth – has predominated in Western culture ever since Wordsworth's time. With writers of the twentieth century, the unconscious heirs of a century of commitment to it, the attitude is a habit rather than a conscious theory (there are exceptions like Wallace Stevens), an 'unexamined major postulate'. Ernest Hemingway's Tintern Abbey country is up in Michigan, somewhere near the Two-Hearted River; Faulkner's is the Big Woods of northern Mississippi.

Fitzgerald's was the urban version of this attitude. He had his feelings for physical nature, but it was always a feeling for the lawns and gardens of estates in Princeton or on Long Island or on the

The dinner party at the Buchanans' from Paramount's 1949 film of *The Great Gatsby*, in which Alan Ladd played Gatsby. This still shows Daisy Buchanan (Betty Field) and Jordan Baker (Ruth Hussey) in the Buchanans' drawing room.

Riviera. He even felt the universal human response to the seasons as a phenomenon of the urban world. A typical paragraph of *The Great Gatsby* will begin, 'Already it was deep summer on roadhouse roofs and in front of wayside garages, where new red gas-pumps sat out in pools of light. . . .' About the objects of this urban world Fitzgerald never forgot anything with which experience had associated his feelings. When he says that '*Three O'Clock in the Morning*, a neat, sad little waltz of that year was drifting out the open door' of Gatsby's house, you may be sure that 'that year' is not merely a poignant reminder of how quickly time passes; it is also a precise identification of the year *Three O'Clock in the Morning* was in fact popular. Fitzgerald lived, as Malcolm Cowley once put it, in a room full of clocks and calendars. This impulse to cling to the exact time and place of an experience, is, of course, also recognizably romantic. Time's fell hand, which will take my love away, has nagged the romantic imagination since the beginning.

Fitzgerald fully shared the romantic anxiety about time; Keats – the Keats of 'Bright Star' and 'Ode on a Grecian Urn' as well as the Keats of the nightingale's tender night – was his favourite poet. But he always expressed this feeling too in terms of the objects of his urban world rather than of the romantics' rural one; in this sense his imagination was very pure. Like the romantic, however, Fitzgerald cared only for what he had felt deeply, and for the times and places in which he had done so. He wrote exclusively about himself and about what had happened to him, not because he was egotistical in the bad sense, but because what he knew best and was most deeply moved by was what had happened to himself.

Unlike most of the great traditional romantics, though like many recent American ones, Fitzgerald was little given to a wise passiveness. He had a powerful impulse to realize his dream here and now, and it went almost without saying – though he eventually learned to practice a superficial irony about this attitude – that the way to do that was in the materials made available to him by the life of his time, by what he would later call a vast, vulgar, meretricious beauty. In a characteristic American – perhaps even Middle Western – way he was ambitious, passionately confident that he could do anything he wanted to if he only tried hard enough, and sure that he could take risks and live as dangerously as he chose because he was immune to moral destruction. 'I want to be the greatest writer that ever lived, don't you?' he said to Edmund Wilson when they were under-graduates. At the end of her novel about their lives, Zelda has her heroine say, 'We grew up founding our dreams on the infinite promise of American advertising. I *still* believe that one can learn to

The kind of advertisements Zelda had in mind (these two date from 1925 and 1927) when she had her heroine say in *Save Me the Waltz*, 'We grew up founding our dreams on the infinite promise of American advertising.'

play the piano by mail and that mud will give you a perfect com-
plexion.' 'Can't repeat the past?' Gatsby cries incredulously. 'Why
of course you can!'

As a result of this ambition, Fitzgerald looked for the realization of
his 'great dream' in the world he found himself in. His paradise was
always – if the other side of where he was – here and now. He kept
finding it, momentarily, in some 'bright rosey-colored space, fragilely
bound into the house by French windows at either end' on Long
Island; at a dinner party at the Murphys' Villa America at Antibes,
when the Murphys would begin 'suddenly to warm and glow and
expand. . . . And for a moment the faces turned up to them were like
the faces of poor children at a Christmas tree'; in a ghost-haunted
moment in an unfinished house at Malibu. Mostly, to be sure, it
eluded him; but '. . . no matter – tomorrow we will run faster, stretch
out our arms farther. . . . And one fine morning –'

But whether it was paradise or not, the physical world in which the
drama of his personal experience was played out was always intensely
important to him. In a sense, as Sara Murphy once pointed out to him
in a moment of irritation, he didn't 'really know anything at all about
people' or places; for him they were always bit-players and sets for a
drama that was going on inside himself. But he was determined that
they should be so concrete and particular, so 'real', that they could not
be distinguished from reality. Mrs Murphy's irritated remark was
made to him after she had stood all she could of Fitzgerald's information-
gathering cross-examination that covered everything from the
Murphys' income to their sexual habits. Thus it comes about that the
world of Fitzgerald's fiction is both rich in the particulars of American
life in his time – to the point where he has been mistaken for a mere
social historian – and at the same time a sort of dream-vision, the
projection of a passionate and limitlessly idealistic conception of the
possibilities of life.

As a consequence, the relations between Fitzgerald's personal life
and his novels are specially important. A knowledge of his life goes
much further than with most writers to help us understand his work,
if only because the gap between the unenchanted vision of the people,
the places, the cars, the clothes, the appurtenances of life that we get
from the camera or from a social historian, and the enchanted but 'real'
vision of those things Fitzgerald gives us is a measure of his achievement.

Fitzgerald once called himself a first-rate writer who had never
written anything but second-rate books. This is an exaggeration, but
on the right side, an example of Fitzgerald's remarkable capacity for
being honest about himself. 'In a *small* way,' he wrote Max Perkins
near the end of his life, with the terrifyingly casual past tense characteristic of him at this time, 'I was an original.' In saying so, he was
plainly thinking of his contribution to the popular culture of the 1920s,
the definition in his early work of the Jazz Age, as it was called – as he

indeed had named it. This he had done, in a popular, even naive but quite often genuine way not to be despised ('A book which college boys really read', as Glenway Wescott observed of *This Side of Paradise*, 'is a rare thing, not to be dismissed idly or in a moment of severe sophistication').

At the start of his career, then, with all his emotional energy and enthusiasm and all his capacity for headlong commitment to the world he was sure he could make expressive of his feelings, he plunged into the life of the early 1920s, simultaneously living it and writing about it in a way certain to exhaust anyone, at once determined to hold nothing back and convinced that every commitment was an irre-coverable expenditure of emotional energy. Part of him was eager for experience, acutely conscious that time was passing and that there was none to waste. This was the Fitzgerald who always went too far – flunking out of Princeton because he would not spare any time at all for academic work from the world of the Triangle Club and social success; throwing money around New York in an ecstasy of spending, so that even his large income of the early Twenties could not keep him from bankruptcy; insisting, when he lived on the Riviera, on excitement even at the risk of death.

Part of him knew from the start, however, that the very thing that made him run so hard made running hard futile; however fast he ran, time ran faster.

> For one, eternal morning of desire
> Passes to time and earthy afternoon,

he said when he left Princeton. Time, carrying you inescapably from the morning of desire's anticipation to the earthy afternoon of fulfill-ment, destroyed all that you cared about most. (This feeling is some-times mistaken for priggishness or even a revulsion from sex.) One of the things he remembered most vividly from the days of his early success in New York was that 'riding in a taxi one afternoon between very tall buildings under a mauve and rosy sky . . . I began to bawl because I had everything I wanted and knew I would never be so happy again.'

The Fitzgerald whose early life and work so perfectly exemplified the Jazz Age was, then, a figure of some significance in the social history of the early Twenties. But even then, young as he was, he stood out among the writers of novels about Flaming Youth – the Cyril Humes, the Dorothy Spearses, the Katherine Brushes – because there was something more than this inside him. Without ever trying to reject the life that was his familiar material, without even trying to discard any of the attitudes and values with which he had begun, but only trying to refine and deepen his awareness of the world he lived in, Fitzgerald became, with *The Great Gatsby* (1925), a major American writer. Through the rest of his career, blurred and confused though it was by the disasters of his personal life, he continued to be that. *Tender Is the Night* (1934) is a novel filled with technical faults, partly the result of its having been rewritten many times and having bits and pieces from earlier versions patched into it, partly as a result of the book's having been written, in Fitzgerald's phrase, 'entirely on stimulant'. *The Last Tycoon* was left incomplete at Fitzgerald's death. The short stories of his last years were often hastily written by an exhausted man. Nevertheless, *Tender Is the Night* is a more profound book than *The Great Gatsby*; *The Last Tycoon* is, in the richness of its verbal texture, superior to anything Fitzgerald ever wrote; and, with one or two exceptions, all Fitzgerald's major stories were written in the period from 1930 on, many of them at the very end of it.

Perhaps, nonetheless, Fitzgerald was in a sense right when he suggested that he had never made what he should have of his talent. Heroic as his persistence in writing his best was, he lived in a way that made it impossible for him to develop his talent systematically; and it is not easy to believe he could have done otherwise. There was something intimately related to his capacity to create – or at least to the conception of life in terms of which he was bound to create – that required him to wear himself out, to risk self-destruction, in the cultivation of experience. This may not be, in an absolute sense, a necessary connection. But it clearly was necessary for Fitzgerald, as it is perhaps for everyone committed to the cult of experience – to say nothing of those not only committed to it but confident that they can make experience over into what they want it to be. ('Life', Fitzgerald had believed, 'was something you dominated if you were any good.')

It is our awareness of this necessity that gives to Fitzgerald's inextricably entangled life and career its special fascination: the life that seems so inimical to the career, so destructive of Fitzgerald's talent, is nonetheless necessary to its fulfillment. How else save by direct experience can the man for whom nothing is real except what he had felt strongly about know the world or acquire the material for fiction? The risks Fitzgerald ran with such unanticipated and disastrous results were, for him, necessary to the development of his talent, however destructive they also were of that talent.

In any event, it is true that his life and works are mirror images of one another, not literally – as if he had written mere autobiography or sought to live the life he dreamed for his heroes – but in the values he and his heroes both sought to realize and in the acts of life those values dictated. Fitzgerald's much admired friend, Hemingway – or at least Hemingway's hero, Jake Barnes – once said that only bullfighters live their lives all the way up. The exception may well be questionable. But at least romantics like Fitzgerald and Hemingway – as much of the time as they can and in spite of the romantic irony of Jake Barnes and Nick Carroway – do try to live their lives all the way up and feel somehow cheated and betrayed when they cannot do so. This enterprise is their glory and perhaps the source of their imaginative energy as well as the cause of their destruction, whether – as in Fitzgerald's case – slowly from drinking or – as in Hemingway's case – quickly by shotgun.

The 'ironic paperweight' that stood on Fitzgerald's desk during the last years of his life (see p. 87 above).

CHRONOLOGY

1896 Francis Scott Key Fitzgerald is born in St Paul, Minnesota, on 24 September.

1898– Fitzgerald's father works for
1908 Procter and Gamble in Syracuse and Buffalo, New York.

1908 The Fitzgeralds move back to St Paul, where Mr Fitzgerald works as a wholesale grocery salesman. Fitzgerald is sent to St Paul Academy, a private boys' school.

1911 Fitzgerald is sent to Newman Academy in Hackensack, New Jersey, where he is unpopular.

1913 Fitzgerald enters Princeton and, though only 5 feet 7 inches tall and weighing 138 pounds, he tries to make the football team. He is more successful with the Triangle Club, a socially influential organization that produces an annual musical show. He quickly gets into academic difficulties but manages to pass his exams at the year's end.

1914 Fitzgerald's sophomore year. His libretto for the Triangle Club, *Fie! Fie! Fi-Fi!* is accepted, but his academic situation makes him ineligible for the show's Christmas tour. He spends the vacation in St Paul, where he meets his generation's most beautiful debutante, Ginevra King, at a dance at the St Paul Town and Country Club. She will be the model for Isabelle in his novel *This Side of Paradise*.

1915 Fitzgerald is elected to a socially important Club, Cottage, and becomes secretary of the Triangle Club, with every prospect of being president in his senior year. But in June he fails three subjects and, in the fall, fails the make-up examinations in two of them. He thus again is ineligible for the Triangle Club's show, this year a musical play called *The Evil Eye*, written by Edmund Wilson, with lyrics by F. Scott Fitzgerald. In November it becomes clear that he will be dropped from the university at the end of the year and he decides to leave, thus missing the spring when the elections to all the offices he had hoped to win take place.

1916 Fitzgerald returns to Princeton to repeat his junior year. He substitutes a literary career for his lost social one, becoming a close friend of Edmund Wilson and John Peale Bishop and writing extensively for the undergraduate literary magazine. He completes the first version of *This Side of Paradise*.

1917 In October Fitzgerald leaves Princeton to join the army as a second lieutenant. During his training he rewrites his novel; it is turned down for the second time.

1918 While stationed at Camp Sheridan, near Montgomery, Alabama, he meets and falls in love with Zelda Sayre.

1919 Fitzgerald is demobilized in February and goes to New York to earn his fortune. The best he can do is a minor job in advertising. Zelda breaks their engagement, Fitzgerald quits his job and returns to St Paul to rewrite his novel once more. It is accepted by Scribner's in September and the engagement is renewed.

1920 *This Side of Paradise* is published in March and Fitzgerald and Zelda are married in April. They become famous figures about New York.

1921 During the summer they make their first trip abroad. *Flappers and Philosophers* is published. Their child, Frances Fitzgerald, is born in St Paul, 26 October.

1922 Fitzgerald's second novel, *The Beautiful and Damned*, is published in March, *Tales of the Jazz Age* in September. In October the Fitzgeralds move back to New York, to Great Neck, Long Island.

1923 Fitzgerald spends most of the year on a play, *The Vegetable*, which opens in Atlantic City in November and is a hopeless failure. He spends the winter turning out popular stories to pay his debts.

1924 The Fitzgeralds decide to move to France to save money and settle at St Raphaël on the Riviera. In September Zelda has a brief but serious love affair with a French aviator. They go to Rome for the winter.

1925 *The Great Gatsby* is published on 11 April; it is a critical but not a financial success. In May the Fitzgeralds come to Paris for a summer of '1000 parties and no work'. In August they go to Antibes.

1926 In February *All the Sad Young Men* is published and the successful dramatic version of *The Great Gatsby* opens in New York. Fitzgerald works with Hemingway over *The Sun Also Rises*. They spend the summer at Antibes and return to America in December.

1927 Fitzgerald goes to Hollywood and writes an unproduced script for Constance Talmadge. He meets Lois Moran, on whom he will later base Rosemary Hoyt of *Tender Is the Night*. In March they take a house called Ellerslie near Wilmington, Del.

1928 Zelda takes up ballet dancing with obsessive intensity and they decide to spend the summer in Paris. They return to Ellerslie in September. Both are drinking heavily.

1929 They go to Paris again in the spring and to the Riviera for the summer.

1930 Zelda grows anxious over her failure to get any offers to dance professionally and, after a trip to Algiers, breaks down in April. She is hospitalized for the rest of the year in Switzerland.

1931 Zelda begins to recover in the spring and by September is well enough to go home to Montgomery, where she stays while Fitzgerald goes to Hollywood to do a script of Katherine Brush's *Red-Headed Woman*.

1932 Zelda's father dies and Zelda breaks down again. She is taken to Johns Hopkins for treatment and Fitzgerald moves into a house called La Paix at Rodgers Forge.

1933 Through this year they struggle with Zelda's illness and Fitzgerald's alcoholism and Fitzgerald finally completes *Tender Is the Night*.

1934 Zelda breaks down for the third time. Though she has better and worse spells for the remainder of her life, she is never wholly well again. By the year's end Fitzgerald is in despair, in severe financial difficulties, without hope for Zelda's recovery, and drinking heavily.

1935 *Taps at Reveille* is published in the spring. Fitzgerald flees to North Carolina and tries to cure himself. Back in Baltimore in the fall he moves to the Cambridge Arms, opposite the Johns Hopkins campus.

1936 Fitzgerald publishes the 'Crack-Up' articles describing his own collapse. 'Me caring for no one and nothing,' he says privately.

1937 Fitzgerald returns to North Carolina and tries once more to pull himself together. In July he is well enough to go to Hollywood as a script writer, where he works hard for the rest of the year. He meets Sheilah Graham and falls in love with her.

1938 Fitzgerald writes a script for *Three Comrades*, has it gutted by the producer and loses all hope of a satisfying career in Hollywood. He collaborates with Budd Schulberg on *Winter Carnival*.

1939 Fitzgerald gives up all but occasional movie work and begins to write stories for *Esquire*. He begins *The Last Tycoon*.

1940 Fitzgerald does scattered movie work, including a script of his own story, 'Babylon Revisited', that is never produced. In November he returns to *The Last Tycoon*. Late that month he has a heart attack. He tries desperately to finish *The Last Tycoon* but has completed only six chapters when he has a final, fatal heart attack on 21 December. On 27 December he is buried in the Rockville, Maryland, Union Cemetery. Zelda was buried beside him when she died in 1948.

BIBLIOGRAPHY

BOOKS BY FITZGERALD

This Side of Paradise, New York: Charles Scribner's Sons, 1920

Flappers and Philosophers, New York: Charles Scribner's Sons, 1921

The Beautiful and Damned, New York: Charles Scribner's Sons, 1922

Tales of the Jazz Age, New York: Charles Scribner's Sons, 1922

The Vegetable or From President to Postman, New York: Charles Scribner's Sons, 1923

The Great Gatsby, New York: Charles Scribner's Sons, 1925

All the Sad Young Men, New York: Charles Scribner's Sons, 1926

Tender Is the Night, New York: Charles Scribner's Sons, 1934

Taps at Reveille, New York: Charles Scribner's Sons, 1935

The Last Tycoon, edited by Edmund Wilson, New York: Charles Scribner's Sons, 1941

The Crack-Up, edited by Edmund Wilson, Norfolk, Connecticut: New Directions, 1945

The Stories of F. Scott Fitzgerald, A Selection of 28 Stories With an Introduction by Malcolm Cowley, New York: Charles Scribner's Sons, 1951

Tender Is the Night [the Revised Version], With an Introduction by Malcolm Cowley, New York: Charles Scribner's Sons, 1951

Afternoon of an Author, A Selection of Uncollected Stories and Essays, With an Introduction and Notes by Arthur Mizener, Princeton, New Jersey: Princeton University Library, 1957

The Letters of F. Scott Fitzgerald, edited by Andrew Turnbull, New York: Charles Scribner's Sons, 1963

Dear Scott/Dear Max: The Fitzgerald–Perkins Correspondence, edited by John Kuehl and Jackson R. Bryer, New York: Charles Scribner's Sons, 1971

The Pat Hobby Series, edited by Arnold Gingrich, New York: Charles Scribner's Sons, 1962

The Apprentice Fiction of F. Scott Fitzgerald, 1909–1917, edited by John Kuehl, New Brunswick, New Jersey: Rutgers University Press, 1965

The Price Was High: The Last Uncollected Stories of F. Scott Fitzgerald, Volume 1, New York: Harcourt Brace Jovanovich, 1979

The Bodley Head Scott Fitzgerald, in six volumes (London, 1958–63), contains all Fitzgerald's novels, sixty-two of his short stories, seven essays, and a selection of his letters to his daughter.

BOOKS ABOUT FITZGERALD,
A SELECTION

Andrew Turnbull, *Scott Fitzgerald,* New York: Charles Scribner's Sons, 1962

F. Scott Fitzgerald, A Collection of Critical Essays, edited by Arthur Mizener, Englewood Cliffs, New Jersey: Prentice-Hall 1963

Arthur Mizener, *The Far Side of Paradise, A Biography of F. Scott Fitzgerald,* Revised Edition, Boston: Houghton, Mifflin Company, 1965

Henry Dan Piper, *F. Scott Fitzgerald, A Critical Portrait,* New York: Holt, Rinehart and Winston, 1965

Nancy W. Milford, *Zelda Fitzgerald, A Biography,* New York: Harper and Row, 1970

Matthew J. Bruccoli, *Some Sort of Epic Grandeur: The Life of F. Scott Fitzgerald,* London: Hodder and Stoughton, 1981

André Le Vot, *F. Scott Fitzgerald: A Biography,* Paris: Juillard, 1979, and London: Allen Lane, 1984

NOTES ON THE PICTURES

Frontispiece F. Scott Fitzgerald; studio portrait. Photograph in the collection of the author.

5 Summit Avenue, the main residential street of St Paul, *c.* 1916. F. Scott Fitzgerald lived with his family at the less fashionable end of the street at this time. Minnesota Historical Society.

6 F. Scott Fitzgerald aged two, in front of 479–480 Laurel Avenue, St Paul, where the Fitzgerald family were living at that time, with Mrs Fitzgerald in the background. Photograph in the collection of Miss Alice C. Brill, St Paul.

F. Scott Fitzgerald, *c.* 1902. Photograph in the collection of the author.

7 F. Scott Fitzgerald and his father, Edward Fitzgerald, 1899. Photograph in the collection of the author.

Mary Fitzgerald; F. Scott Fitzgerald's mother, in early middle age. Photograph in the collection of the author.

8 The Christian Student; statue by Daniel Chester French for Princeton University campus. Princeton University.

9 Sanford B. White; captain of the Princeton University football team in 1911. Princeton University Library.

Hobey Baker, 1911; he became the captain of the Princeton University football team in 1913, the year

F. Scott Fitzgerald was accepted for Princeton. Princeton University Library.

10 Princeton *v.* Yale, 1913. Princeton University Library.

11 599 Summit Avenue, St Paul; the house in which the Fitzgeralds were living when Scott was at Princeton University. Minneapolis Star and Tribune.

12 F. Scott Fitzgerald aged fifteen. Princeton University Library (F. Scott Fitzgerald Papers).

13 Ina Claire; portrait from *Vanity Fair*, February 1914. Periodicals Division, Library of Congress, Washington, D.C.

14 F. Scott Fitzgerald in the Elizabethan Dramatic Club's production *The Coward*, 1913. Princeton University Library (F. Scott Fitzgerald Papers).

15 F. Scott Fitzgerald on the Newman Academy football team, 1912. Princeton University Library (F. Scott Fitzgerald Papers).

16 Panoramic view of the Princeton University campus, 1913–17; engraving. Princeton University Library.

17 Blair Hall, Princeton University. United States Information Service.

Princeton *v.* Dartmouth, 1914; the game which opened the Palmer Stadium. Princeton University Library.

18 John Peale Bishop as an undergraduate at Princeton, *c.*1915.
Princeton University Library.

Edmund Wilson as an undergraduate at Princeton, *c.*1915.
Princeton University Library.

19 *The Evil Eye*, the Triangle Club's
production for 1915–16 written by
Edmund Wilson with lyrics by
F. Scott Fitzgerald; cover. Collection of the author.

20 Holder Court on Princeton
campus, where Edmund Wilson
had his rooms; pen drawing.
Princeton University Library.

21 F. Scott Fitzgerald and Jimmy
Dunn at Princeton, *c.*1915, with
an inscription by Fitzgerald below.
Photograph in the collection of the
author.

22 F. Scott Fitzgerald, 1915. Photograph in the collection of the author.

24 *Fie! Fie! Fi-Fi!*, the Triangle
Club's production for 1914–15
written by F. Scott Fitzgerald
although credited to Walker Ellis;
scene from the second act. Princeton
University Library.

Fie! Fie! Fi-Fi!, the Triangle
Club's production for 1914–15.
Cover of the score. Princeton
University Library.

25 F. Scott Fitzgerald as a chorus girl;
publicity photo for *The Evil Eye*,
the Triangle Club's production for
1915–16, and for subsequent Triangle Club productions; cutting
from *The New York Times*, October
1915. Collection of the author.

26 'The Spire and The Gargoyle'; a
short story by F. Scott Fitzgerald on
the opening page of Princeton
University's *Nassau Literary Magazine*, February 1917. Princeton
University Library.

St Paul Town and Country Club;
where F. Scott Fitzgerald met
Ginevra King on 4 January 1915.
Minnesota Historical Society.

27 Ginevra King *c.*1915; photograph
in a scrapbook record compiled by
F. Scott Fitzgerald. Princeton University Library (F. Scott Fitzgerald
Papers).

28 Ginevra King *c.*1915; photograph
in a scrapbook record compiled by
F. Scott Fitzgerald. Princeton University Library (F. Scott Fitzgerald
Papers).

29 The Pyne Estate on Mercer Street,
Princeton, 1913–17. Princeton
University Library.

The Cottage Club, Princeton; F.
Scott Fitzgerald was a member,
1916–17. Princeton University
Library.

30 *Safety First*; the Triangle Club's
production for 1916–17 written by
F. Scott Fitzgerald's room mate
John Biggs, with lyrics by Fitzgerald; poster. Princeton University Library.

31 Lake Forest, November 1916.
Courtesy Chicago Historical
Society.

32 Henry Strater as an undergraduate
at Princeton, *c.*1915. Princeton
University Library.

David Bruce as an undergraduate
at Princeton, *c.*1915. Princeton
University Library.

34 Dean Gauss; studio portrait by
Bachrach.

'Now what shall we commence?';
cover of *Life* magazine, 2 June 1927,
by J. L. Holton. Periodicals Division, Library of Congress, Washington, D.C.

51 'The Dance-Mad Younger Set',
1925; cartoon by John Held, Jr. By
kind permission of Mrs John Held,
Jr.

A Charleston competition under
way in New York, 1926. United
Press International (U.K.) Ltd.

52 View of the Plaza Hotel, New
York, from Central Park; undated
photograph by Byron, probably
1920s. The Byron Collection,
Museum of the City of New York.

53 Advertisement for telephones,
c. 1900. American Telephone and
Telegraph Company, New York.

'Berenice's Mother bobs her hair';
cartoon from *Vanity Fair*, July 1921,
parodying illustrations and F. Scott
Fitzgerald's story 'Berenice Bobs
Her Hair', then in *The Saturday
Evening Post*. Periodicals Division,
Library of Congress, Washington,
D.C.

54 The Pulitzer Fountain at West
58th Street and Fifth Avenue, New
York, 1916. Museum of the City
of New York.

The Pulitzer Fountain and the
Plaza Hotel, New York; drawing
from *Vanity Fair*, February 1922.
Periodicals Division, Library of
Congress, Washington, D.C.

56 F. Scott Fitzgerald wearing Norfolk jacket, 1921. Photograph in
the collection of the author.

57 Zelda Fitzgerald; studio portrait,
1921. Photograph in the collection
of the author.

58 Zelda Fitzgerald in a hotel room;
photograph entitled 'First trip
abroad', 1921. Photograph in the
collection of Mrs Clinton Grove
Smith.

Inscription by Zelda on the back
of a postcard of the Fitzgeralds in
Venice. Postcard in the collection
of the author.

F. Scott Fitzgerald and Zelda in a
gondola in Venice, 1921. Postcard
in the collection of the author.

59 'The New Generation in Literature'; a page from *Vanity Fair*,
February 1922, of young American
writers, including John Gilbert
Seldes, John Peale Bishop, Donald
Ogden Stewart, John Dos Passos,
John V. A. Weaver, John Farrar,
Stephen Vincent Benet, Edmund
Wilson and F. Scott Fitzgerald.
Periodicals Division, Library of
Congress, Washington, D.C.

60 Zelda Fitzgerald at White Bear
Lake, 1922. Photograph in the
collection of the author.

The Beautiful and Damned by F.
Scott Fitzgerald; jacket by W. E.
Hill, 1922. Collection of the author.

61 Zelda Fitzgerald with her daughter,
Scottie, at White Bear Lake during
the summer of 1922. Photograph
in the collection of Mrs Clinton
Grove Smith.

Zelda Fitzgerald on the quay at
White Bear Lake in the summer of
1922. Photograph in the collection
of the author.

F. Scott Fitzgerald on the quay at
White Bear Lake in the summer of
1922. Photograph in the collection
of the author.

62 Rolls-Royce Silver Cloud, 1922
model. The Fitzgeralds owned a

second-hand Rolls-Royce in 1922. Photo: Rolls-Royce Motors Ltd.

63 Paul Whiteman and his band in the 1920s. They played regularly at the Palais Royal, a fashionable New York night club. Radio Times Hulton Picture Library.

'The Diamond as Big as the Ritz' by F. Scott Fitzgerald; cover for *The Smart Set*, the magazine in which the story first appeared, June 1922. Collection of the author.

64 Zelda Fitzgerald, *c.* 1921-23. Photograph in the collection of the author.

65 An illustration for 'The Millionaire's Girl', published in *The Saturday Evening Post*, 17 May 1930. Reprinted with permission from *The Saturday Evening Post* copyright The Curtis Publishing Company.

Ring Lardner; caricature by Covarrubias in *Vanity Fair*, July 1925. Periodicals Division, Library of Congress, Washington, D.C.

66 Ring Lardner with his family; photograph from *Vanity Fair*, March 1923. Periodicals Division, Library of Congress, Washington, D.C.

67 Three versions of a galley of *The Great Gatsby* starting from the beginning of the Plaza Hotel episode, showing corrections by F. Scott Fitzgerald. Princeton University Library (F. Scott Fitzgerald Papers).

69 Inscription on a first edition of *The Great Gatsby* by F. Scott Fitzgerald for Carmel Myers. Collection of the author.

Carmel Myers in M.G.M.'s *Ben Hur*, filmed in Rome in 1924-25. National Film Archive.

70 *The Great Gatsby* by F. Scott Fitzgerald; dust jacket. Collection of the author.

71 Edsel Ford's Hispano Suiza; photograph in *Vanity Fair*, April 1923. Periodicals Division, Library of Congress, Washington, D.C.

72 F. Scott Fitzgerald with Zelda and Scottie, 1925. Photograph in the collection of the author.

73 Café du Dome, Paris, *c.* 1925. The Fitzgeralds were in Paris in 1925. Collection Viollet, Paris.

74 La Place Nationale, Antibes, *c.* 1925. The Fitzgeralds spent the summer of 1925 in Antibes. Photo: N. D. Roger-Viollet.

75 The Murphys and the MacLeishes in Vienna during the 1920s. Photograph in the collection of Honoria Murphy Donnelly.

Rudolph Valentino. National Film Archive.

76 The Murphys' house, 'Villa America', at Antibes. Photograph in the collection of Honoria Murphy Donnelly.

Gerald and Sara Murphy on the beach at Antibes. Photograph in the collection of Honoria Murphy Donnelly.

77 Ernest Hemingway in Paris, *c.* 1925; study by Man Ray. Photo: Ullstein Bilderdienst.

78 Lois Moran in a film role during the 1920s. F. Scott Fitzgerald met her in Hollywood in 1927. National Film Archive.

John Barrymore; photograph from *Vanity Fair*, January 1920. F. Scott Fitzgerald met him in Hollywood in 1927. National Film Archive.

79 F. Scott Fitzgerald and Richard Barthelmess on a Hollywood set in January 1927. Photograph in the collection of the author.

80 Constance Talmadge; from a contemporary postcard. F. Scott Fitzgerald worked on a script for United Artists starring Constance Talmadge, but it was rejected.

81 Zelda Fitzgerald in ballet costume at Ellerslie, 1929. Photograph in the collection of the author.

82 F. Scott Fitzgerald and Zelda arriving at *Dinner at Eight* in Baltimore, 1932. Photograph in the collection of the author.

83 Motor car for sale in New York during the Depression, 1929. United Press International (U.K.) Ltd.

84 Zelda Fitzgerald, 1929; studio portrait by the Montgomerys. Photograph in the collection of the author.

Zelda Fitzgerald, 1931; photograph entitled 'Recovered', in the Fitzgerald album. Photograph in the collection of the author.

85 Self-portrait by Zelda Fitzgerald, early 1940s; watercolour. Princeton University Library (F. Scott Fitzgerald Papers).

86 Zelda Fitzgerald and Scottie on a beach, *c.* 1933. Photograph in the collection of the author.

87 F. Scott Fitzgerald in his study at 'La Paix', Baltimore, *c.* 1933.

Photo: Cecilia Norfolk Eareckson. Collection of the author.

88 'La Paix', the Fitzgeralds' house in Baltimore. Photograph courtesy the Baltimore Sunpapers.

89 F. Scott Fitzgerald and Zelda with their furniture on the front lawn of 'La Paix', Baltimore, after a fire which Zelda had inadvertently started, 1933–34. Photograph in the collection of the author.

91 Zelda Fitzgerald painting at 'La Paix', Baltimore, 1933–34. Photograph in the collection of the author.

F. Scott Fitzgerald fishing, *c.* 1933. Photograph in the collection of the author.

92 F. Scott Fitzgerald at 1307 Park Avenue, Baltimore, 1934. Photograph in the collection of the author.

93 *Tender Is the Night* by F. Scott Fitzgerald; illustration by Edward Shenston on page 9 of the first edition, 1934. British Museum. Photo: R. B. Fleming.

Tender Is the Night by F. Scott Fitzgerald; illustration by Edward Shenston on page 51 of the first edition, 1934. British Museum. Photo: R. B. Fleming.

94 Francis Scott Key monument, Baltimore. Francis Scott Key was a distant cousin of F. Scott Fitzgerald's paternal grandmother. Camera Press Ltd.

95 *Taps at Reveille* by F. Scott Fitzgerald, 1935; jacket. Collection of the author.

96 Grove Park Inn, Asheville, North Carolina, where F. Scott Fitzgerald stayed 1936–37. The hotel

has been altered since Fitzgerald stayed there, and this photograph shows it as it is today. United States Travel Service.

97 F. Scott Fitzgerald and a companion duck-shooting near Asheville, North Carolina, on 12 January 1936. Photograph in the collection of the author.

99 F. Scott Fitzgerald outside the Algonquin Hotel, New York, 1937. Photo: Carl Van Vechten.

100 Irving Thalberg, 1936. Princeton University Library (William Seymour Theater Collection).

F. Scott Fitzgerald in Hollywood, standing before the Garden of Allah, where he lived in 1937. Princeton University Library (F. Scott Fitzgerald Papers).

101 Sheilah Graham aged nineteen. Photograph in the collection of Mrs Sheilah Graham Westbrook.

F. Scott Fitzgerald at the Beverly Hills Tennis Club during the summer of 1937; photograph taken and inscribed by Scottie. Photograph in the collection of the author.

102 F. Scott Fitzgerald and Sheilah Graham in Tijuana, Mexico, early in 1940. Photograph in the collection of Mrs Sheilah Graham Westbrook.

103 *The Three Comrades* (M.G.M.), 1938, starring Robert Young, Robert Taylor, Margaret Sullavan and Franchot Tone; film still. F. Scott Fitzgerald worked on the script. National Film Archive.

104 *Winter Carnival* (Walter Wanger Productions), 1939, starring Ann Sheridan and Richard Carlson; film still. F. Scott Fitzgerald worked on the script until he was fired by Wanger. National Film Archive.

107 The back lot of the M.G.M. studios, *c.* 1935. F. Scott Fitzgerald based descriptions of Monroe Stahr's studios in *The Last Tycoon* on memories of studios like these. National Film Archive.

108 F. Scott Fitzgerald's and Zelda's tombstone in the Rockville Union Cemetery, Maryland. Photograph courtesy Baltimore Sunpapers.

110 *The Great Gatsby* (Paramount), 1949, starring Alan Ladd, Betty Field and Ruth Hussey; film still with Betty Field as Daisy Buchanan and Ruth Hussey as Jordan Baker. National Film Archive.

111 Advertisement for the United States School of Music, 1925, and an advertisement for Lux soap, 1927.

115 Paperweight which stood on F. Scott Fitzgerald's desk during the last years of his life, now in the possession of the author.

INDEX